Lifestyle of Happiness

What to Take Away From Today's Lifestyle Trends

By Sofie Bakken

Lifestyle of Happiness

What to Take Away From Today's Lifestyle Trends

By Sofie Bakken

Disclaimer:

Although the author has made every effort to ensure that the information in this book was correct at press time, the author does not assume and hereby disclaim any liability to any party for any loss, damage, or disruption caused by errors or omissions, whether such errors or omissions result from negligence, accident, or any other cause.
This book is not intended as a substitute for the medical advice of physicians. The reader should regularly consult a physician in matters relating to his/her health and particularly concerning any symptoms that may require diagnosis or medical attention.

**Lifestyle of Happiness
What To Take Away From Today's Lifestyle Trends**

BN Publishing

© 2021 by Sofie Bakken
All Rights Reserved.
ISBN: 978-8-1950-8746-4

TABLE OF CONTENTS

TABLE OF CONTENTS 5
FOREWORD 9
INTRODUCTION 11
CHAPTER 1 UNDERSTANDING HAPPINESS 15
    The different meanings of life 15
    Finding happiness 22
    Ordinary life vs meaningful life 25
CHAPTER 2 DIFFERENT LIFESTYLES IN THE WORLD 29
    Europe 34
        Niksen 35
        Hygge 37
        Friluftsliv 38
        Coorie 39
    North America 41
        Cocooning 41
        Augmented and Programmed Lives 42
        Culture of Production and Sharing 42
        Resilient and Proactive Citizens 43

- The Quest for Purpose 43
- South America 45
- Antarctica 48
- Australia 50
  - The Aussie Way of Life 50
- Africa 54
- Asia 55
  - Mottainai 57
- Global lifestyles: an overview 62
- Life after COVID-19 63
  - Reset your priorities 64
  - Take frequent breaks 64
  - Seek help 65
  - Be considerate 65
  - Look after yourself 65
- CHAPTER 3 WHAT DETERMINES YOUR LIFESTYLE? . 67
- Goals 68
- Responsibilities 69
- Nature of work 70
- Personality 70
- Living conditions 71
- Set of beliefs 71
- Strength of willpower 72

Learning never stops 73
CHAPTER 4 SOME HABITS TO INCREASE HAPPINESS 77
Exercise 79
Spend time with nature 81
Smile a lot 82
Stay productive 82
Eat healthy food 84
Socialize 85
Adequate sleep 86
Whine less, thank more 88
Be kind 88
Focus on mental health 89
Maintain a daily journal 91
Be organized 92
Forgive more 93
Strengthen your faith 94
Listen to your inner voice 95
Find an outlet for negative emotions 97
Develop a sense of humor 98
Have a pet 98
Get creative 99
Read more books 100
Get that adrenaline rush 101

CHAPTER 5 THE FUTURE OF THE WORLD 103
    Upcoming trends and the future of the world 103
        Increased technology 105
        Social awareness 105
        Gender equality 106
        Self-reliance 107
        The more frequent occurrence of natural disasters
        107
    Future predictions: an overview 108
    The importance of emotional health 109
CHAPTER 6 FAMOUS PEOPLE ABOUT HAPPINESS..... 113
    Famous Politicians 113
    Sports Personalities 115
    Celebrities and entertainment personalities 117
CONCLUSION 119
REFERENCES 123
OTHER BOOKS BY SOFIE BAKKEN 127
ABOUT SOFIE BAKKEN 129

FOREWORD

I have written a few books on certain specific lifestyle topics like Friluftsliv or Niksen (together with Tess Jansen).

With my most recent book, I covered "Longevity" as this has always been somewhat of a "side topic" when I was occupied with lifestyle trends.

Finally, I felt the desire to write a more comprehensive book on lifestyle trends and so I started looking around to see how people live.

And – it is amazing! There is so much!

However, in the end, I believe – whatever life you live – it always boils town to one word: Happiness. People want to be happy, that's how they live, and that's why they live as they live (if they have the privilege of choosing their lifestyle).

So, my wish for you as a reader of this book is that you may get some inspiration and find your own, personal happiness!

Love, Sofie

INTRODUCTION

The planet earth is more than 4.54 billion years old. It has seen the rise and fall of several generations. It is witness to the gradual progression of life as we know it today.

Each generation goes a step further in enhancing its experience based on the information passed on by the ancestors. The earth is familiar with so many ups and downs that people have always had to encounter. To us, everything may seem incredibly different but as a neutral spectator, this planet can identify the similarities across all generations.

But with everything that is currently happening around us, it is time to question whether we're sustainably living life. Are we taking away too much from the environment without replenishing it? Are the resources going to last long enough for our future generations to live as comfortably as we do?

We often hear that the earth is healing/recovering from something it has suffered in the past. But that recovery is not tantamount to new inhabitable areas being created. It is simply nature's way of giving us a new lease on life.

Thankfully, these small mercies do let us get by to some extent. However, it is only until the next catastrophe occurs. A catastrophe that is often man-made and completely avoidable.

We've seen this in the case of ozone depletion and more of such examples. Human beings often become a cause of nuisance to other living things without fully realizing it. The intentions may not be bad but the consequences are suffered by everybody nonetheless.

Now, we can't single-handedly change the whole system of the world. That is not something within our power. But in our capacity, we have to ensure that we're not endorsing any unhealthy trends.

Coming back to the point of giving back to the planet, you may have heard that you can't pour from an empty cup. If you feel dissatisfied with life yourself, you won't care much about the well-being of any other person or thing. A happy person is better motivated to influence the surroundings positively.

The idea is to change the world, one person, at a time. By focusing on your contentment, you'll be doing a huge favor to your mind and body. Besides, you'll become a more useful person for the people and things around you including the environment.

The act is as selfless as it is selfish. We often forget that our being is just an extension of the world that we live in. Collectively, our well-being reflects in the situation of the planet.

Currently, just like earth's energy is being used up generation by generation, we're being exhausted by our responsibilities with each passing day. And quite similarly, we're not doing anything to replenish the energy.

One may argue that there are activities aimed at rejuvenating the soul. But they're not practiced as often as needed. Moreover, the need to plan with a renewed zest every now and then is often ignored.

Lifestyle of Happiness: What To Take Away From Today's Lifestyle Trends is a text aimed at reminding the readers to keep looking for new reasons to feel happy. It's completely okay to feel lost once in a while but that should never be the reason to give up.

In recent times, happiness is more like an act of defiance with all that the world is currently facing.

You will get to learn about different parts of the world and the lifestyles being observed there. It also includes tips to adopt the right habits to increase happiness. Throughout the entire text, readers would be reminded about the importance of emotional health.

The whole point of this discussion is to look after yourself in more ways instead of just monitoring your physical health. You see, a house needs renovation after every few years. A car needs regular maintenance to operate efficiently.

The funny thing is, the human species may be working more than any of these man-made products but it seldom stops to catch a breath. We've become so busy in our lives that happiness seems like a long-lost dream. Through this text, let's try to relive that dream and make the remaining part of our life a little more colorful.

CHAPTER 1
UNDERSTANDING HAPPINESS

The different meanings of life

Life is often defined as the ability to grow and function. This is the trait that separates living things from nonliving things. Nonliving things, whether they are man-made or natural, cannot perform activities on their own.

So, by this definition, anything that is immobile shall be considered dead or lifeless. Unknowingly, we become a part of this category when we refuse to adapt and evolve with the changing times. Since comfort is an addictive feeling, we prioritize it over the much-needed ability to grow.

Another meaning of the word life is to exist or the state of being. It seems like humans have developed a particular liking for this meaning of the word. After all, we're mostly content with merely being 'alive'.

In this context, being 'alive' is to breathe and have a pulse. We have almost forgotten the aim of progressing further in life. In recent times, survival is the only form of life that we're accustomed to.

Now, we do not wish to demean anybody for trying to remain steadfast despite the extremely challenging circumstances. Such situations can understandably drive somebody towards the option of giving up. So, the current generation's resilience is undoubtedly appreciable.

But when compared with the possibility of enjoying life to the fullest, it does seem like we're being a bit unfair to ourselves. Looking at the other side of the picture, merely surviving does not seem all that heroic. In other words, it seems like we're not utilizing our full potential.

Some numerous theories and faiths encourage human beings to live a better life. Contrary to the popular perception these days, this idea of a better life does not mean having all the luxuries or wealth in the world. It means focusing on virtues and attaining contentment.

Let's briefly discuss some of the world's most popular ideologies that focus on contentment. The Greek philosophy of Stoicism is based on minimizing emotional volatility by thinking logically. It requires you to see reason in all the matters of the universe.

Stoics also believe that virtue is the highest good. Moreover, stoicism emphasizes that if you're virtuous, you naturally feel happy. You don't let life's difficulties affect you and keep focusing on doing good instead.

To sum up the concept of contentment and a forward-looking approach in this philosophy, here are some wise words from the famous Stoic philosopher Epictetus, quoted in the book The Daily Stoic.

> "I am your teacher and you are learning in my school. My aim is to bring you to completion, unhindered, free from compulsive behavior, unrestrained, without shame, free, flourishing, and happy, looking to God in things great and

> small—*your aim is to learn and diligently practice all these things. Why then don't you complete the work, if you have the right aim and I have both the right aim and right preparation? What is missing? ... The work is quite feasible, and is the only thing in our power ... Let go of the past. We must only begin. Believe me and you will see."*

—EPICTETUS

Most of us stop trying to add value to life because we're demotivated by adversities. But as the philosophy suggests, if we uproot the foundations that such negative feelings dwell on, we can succeed in achieving more in life. If personal growth becomes our main objective, others' actions would become irrelevant.

Similarly, a Chinese religion/philosophy known as Taoism is about living in harmony with nature's events. Spontaneity, the main feature of this set of beliefs, means that your conduct would be profound, regardless of external factors. You do not try to control the outcomes but just 'go with the flow'.

Moving on to more widely followed religions, Christianity, Islam, Judaism, etc have all instructed the followers to treat life as a gift. It is not something to be wasted in vanity. One should cherish each and every moment and try to improve oneself continuously.

Most faiths also teach people to submit to their destiny. If you try to understand this message deeply, you will realize that it eliminates half of your worries related to life. For instance, if you didn't get something, you will simply move on believing that it wasn't meant for you.

The Holy Bible states:

> *It is the Lord who directs your life, for each step you take is ordained by God to bring you closer to your destiny.*

(Proverbs 20:24)

A verse from the Holy Quran reads:

> *Say: "Nothing will befall us except what Allah has decreed for us; He is our Protector." Let the believers, then, put all their trust in Allah.*

(9:51)

The Jewish scripture Talmud states:

> *"Do not be daunted by the enormity of the world's grief. Do justly now, love mercy now, walk humbly now. You are not obligated to complete the work, but neither are you free to abandon it."*

In short, these ideologies and faiths suggest that contentment is a choice. Your perception is what defines your reality. You don't need much to be content other than the belief that whatever the universe has given you is sufficient.

Human beings tend to become ungrateful quite easily. If they're given in abundance and left without accountability, they often become corrupt. They become so engrossed in enjoying their blessings that they completely forget that this life is short-lived.

For that, there is the concept of the afterlife. The aforementioned religions believe that there is life after death that will reflect a person's deed during his/her lifetime. People will be sent to heaven if their good deeds exceed their sins or they will be thrown into hell if they have sinned more. This is to emphasize that a person will be held accountable and rewarded/punished for all the actions later.

Hence, the followers learn the lesson of not taking life for granted. They have to make their time on Earth worthy of a blessed afterlife. Moreover, they have to remain virtuous to avoid God's wrath in the afterlife. To merely exist would not earn them this honor.

Some religions like Buddhism and Hinduism have slightly different views about the afterlife. To put it simply, the rebirth or reincarnation of the soul happens here on Earth and this cycle is repeated more than once. The form that the soul takes is dependent on its deeds in the previous life.

So, summarizing the entire discussion about different ideologies and faiths, we can safely say that none of them would deem it sufficient to just sit idle and expect good tidings. One has to actively enhance the quality of life. Learning, growth, and evolution are not just choices but necessities if we understand the true meaning of all these teachings.

Nowadays, religious beliefs are not as rigidly followed as they used to be. Many people are now renouncing religion and moving towards atheism. So, it is important to consider a non-religious view of life as well.

If an individual completely disregards a certain concept, you cannot expect to convince him/her to use the same. What we mean to say is, it would be quite futile to warn a non-believer using religious scriptures or the concept of the afterlife. Atheists need a logical explanation for everything.

This should make them even more inclined to find a purpose in life. They shouldn't simply sit and let 'destiny' take its course. They should determine their fate themselves.

Many renowned personalities in recent history have been atheists. For example, Stephen Hawking was an accomplished physicist, cosmologist, and author who did not believe in God. Yet, his concepts about life were clearer than any hardcore believer.

Hence, we can say that religion or the lack of it does not determine your ability to decode life. It just shapes your perception in a certain way. It would be much more helpful to view things neutrally instead of being anti-/pro-religion.

The perception of life does not just vary according to different religious views. Several other things can change one's outlook. These include age, experiences, culture, society, personality traits, etc.

For example, for a newborn baby, the meaning of life would be laying comfortably in the parent's lap. A teenager would think about various things like education, social life, and plans when considering the purpose of life. An adult would define life as struggling all day long to fulfill his/her responsibilities.

Other than age groups, we can see a stark contrast between the perception of life according to different schools of thought. A philosopher's definition would be opposite to that of a pragmatist. An optimist would always focus on opportunities while a pessimist will think about worst-case scenarios.

However, we have also heard time and again that humanity is a single race. It is unified by certain principles of nature. There are similarities in our lives that act as a binding force for the entire human race.

Feelings and emotions are one of those binding forces. They help us understand each other's perspective even when we do not agree with it completely. One such contagious and relatable feeling is happiness.

We can all identify with the pursuit of happiness in life. Who doesn't want to live with mental peace and positive feelings? In these trying times, almost everyone is looking for solace and emotional stability.

Finding happiness

What is happiness? Receiving an unexpected message from a loved one is happiness. Eating your favorite food is happiness. Listening to some good music is happiness.

At the same time, moving into your dream house after years of hard work is also happiness. Being promoted to the next level in your career is happiness. Finding your soulmate is happiness.

You can experience happiness in a single moment or struggle for years to finally achieve it. So, the feeling isn't bound by time. It knows no boundaries at all. The feeling is quite familiar for people of all age groups, languages, faiths, caste, etc.

In simpler words, it is a universal feeling. It wouldn't be wrong to say that happiness is the most precious thing experienced by living creatures. Remember, the focus here is living creatures, not just humans.

For example, if a mother elephant sees its baby taking the first few steps, it would experience the same joy that the mother of a human baby does when he/she learns to walk. When a bud blooms into a flower, it spreads happiness all around. Hence, we can say that it is a contagious feeling among all kinds of living things. We can pass it on to each other with simple day-to-day actions.

Consider it like the moonlight that illuminates the night sky. It may not eliminate all the darkness but it makes our world a little brighter. And we all need some light to find our way when things get gloomy.

But today, when we look around, we mostly find sorrow and dismay. The planet is experiencing a difficult phase. Human beings, plants, animals, the environment, everyone, and everything is suffering.

As a result, negative emotions have consumed most of the world's population. Sadness, anger, and frustration are more common than ever before. Happiness is desirous but rarely experienced these days.

To feel happy is mostly related to your conduct in life. It is your perception that determines whether an event would make you or break you. A person may lose a job and deem it the end of life while another would strive to achieve an even better position.

Different people have varying ideas about happiness. Some find it in little things while others always want more from life. The feeling may not be too well defined but it is a language that everyone understands equally well.

In recent times, happiness feels somewhat like an achievement. One has to dedicate significant time and effort to feel happy. Otherwise, you just continue to feel miserable about your life.

The problem appears when we start perceiving happiness as a birthright. Of course, the universe has done enough to provide us with a pleasant life, but if we still fail to use it well and also complain about it, that would seem quite ungrateful. Happiness has surely been introduced to us as a possibility but it is up to us whether we choose to explore the feeling or not.

This is just like being provided with a treasure that is hidden somewhere far, far away. Even if unlocking the treasure requires a lot of effort, it certainly isn't a bad deal. It should seem like a fun adventure on its own.

Some treasure hunts provide you with a map and key. While finding happiness may not belong to that category, you're also not left completely unaware of the possible location of the treasure. What we mean to say is, you're allowed to replicate the journey of other explorers who were successful in reaching their destination.

But here comes the tricky part. Not everything that works for another person may work for you as well. So, you need to carefully choose which habits to adopt and which ones to leave out.

More than one-off actions, happiness is achieved through a consistent lifestyle. It is all about picking the right kind of daily habits and surrounding yourself with people and things that bring you joy. There is no set way to live and you can always build a routine according to your preferences.

Finding your purpose helps you remain focused. It eliminates unnecessary worries and stress from life. It is like having a microscopic view of the things that matter the most.

Ordinary life vs meaningful life

You may have often heard that life isn't what happens to you but how you react to it. It is your attitude that decides the level of success you may achieve. Highly successful people are generally known to maintain a positive outlook in life.

But can success be achieved without motivation? If a person does not feel the need to work hard towards his/her goals, can we expect that individual's story to inspire us? Inspiration is drawn from extraordinary achievements, not a half-willed effort to barely survive.

If you're looking to follow the path of a high achiever in any field, you would be interested in the characteristics that led to his/her success. The achiever may have failed multiple times before finally achieving the goal but learning about those failures would not be your main concern. In other words, people are mostly concerned with how you got something right instead of knowing how many times you went wrong.

This urge to find a definite formula for success often deters us from creating a new path for ourselves. We limit ourselves by thinking that the targets set by others are the highest that we may achieve. We seldom consider the possibility that our potential might be even greater.

In every era, only a handful of people dare to break the chain of monotony and do something remarkable. Consequently, only a few people truly live and attain happiness. So much so that their name is forever etched in the books of history.

We're all rushing towards our destination. But the path we take is what determines the quality of our life. Everyone is given a chance at life but not everybody can make it count.

For example, you're traveling to an unknown location. You don't know what you'll find when you get there but you do know two different routes that lead to the destination. One route is plain and uninteresting while the other one has scenic views all along.

Considering the time taken remains the same for both routes, wouldn't you want to use the second one for your journey? The travel might be inevitable but one can at least try to make it a little interesting. This is how one collects pleasant memories to recall at the end of the trip.

Similarly, people can either choose to spend life according to societal norms or try to change their situation for the better. Society doesn't teach you to keep happiness as your main objective. It has many other insignificant parameters to judge people's success.

Trailblazers usually do not care much about customs and norms. They follow their passions and as a result, their life becomes a lot more meaningful than other people. It is usually the ability to prioritize your needs that makes people content and happy.

So, we can say that caring about your happiness also means chasing your dreams. Something that requires immense courage which only a few can muster. This is what distinguishes successful people from unsuccessful ones.

It is quite absurd that in the context of life's journey, the destination we're in a hurry to arrive at is nothing else but death. Of course, death is a certainty and you can't do much about the lifespan that you're destined with. But it wouldn't hurt to make those years worthwhile.

If we look back at history, we would realize that it isn't the accumulation of wealth that immortalized people's names forever, but it is things that are much less materialistic. For example, Helen Keller's refusal to see her disability as a depressing reality. Nelson Mandela's strong opposition to being treated unfairly and made to feel inferior.

The idea is to never settle for a life that is dictated by rules made by other people who are unrelated to you. Nobody knows your strengths and weaknesses, struggles and triumphs, likes, and dislikes better than you. Hence, only you should get to decide how you're supposed to feel and what you need to do in life.

It doesn't matter how long or short the duration of your life is. What makes a difference is the quality of your actions. This is why it is important to adopt a healthy, happy, and growth-inducing lifestyle.

CHAPTER 2
DIFFERENT LIFESTYLES IN THE WORLD

A lifestyle is the set of daily habits that you practice consistently for a significant amount of time. The concept is often confused with the set of beliefs a person has. While beliefs have a great influence on the way you live your life, they do not mean much if they're not translated into actions.

You may care deeply about the planet and preach water conservation to everyone around you. But until and unless you turn the tap off while brushing your teeth, your words would be meaningless. In this example, caring about the planet symbolizes a belief, and turning off the tap is practical action.

So, when we're talking about a lifestyle, it should be clear that we're more concerned with practical steps. Another prerequisite for an action to qualify as a part of an individual's lifestyle is its frequency. Lifestyle consists of regular habits and not something that you might do occasionally.

Exercising once in a blue moon during a sudden spurt of energy will not be considered a part of your lifestyle. However, if you exercise for 20 minutes every morning after waking up, then it would surely count as a daily habit. Even though the activity is the same, whether or not it falls in the category of lifestyle depends on how spontaneous or well thought out it was.

A conscious decision to implement a thought or policy routinely cannot be made without prior contemplation. You don't just get up one day and decide to make drastic changes to your life. Lifestyle is designed after a lot of learning and experience.

When you decide to try new ways of living or to get rid of the old ones, you always carefully consider the pros and cons. You try to align your goals and objectives with your day-to-day habits. In this way, you can achieve greater satisfaction and have a sense of accomplishment.

The concepts such as satisfaction, contentment, and achievement have evolved drastically over the years. Earlier generations would be quite content with necessities like food and shelter. However, these days, it's a completely different story.

The cavemen from the stone age would hunt all day long to provide food for the family. They would encounter countless hurdles in doing so each day. Yet, giving up or getting tired of the routine was never an option.

For shelter, it would suffice to find a natural structure that would offer some protection from the harsh environment. Rocks were made somewhat comfortable for bedding by laying soft leaves on them. The lifestyle was simple, minimalistic, and from a modern person's point of view, quite challenging as well.

Before money was introduced, people used to exchange goods through the barter system. In the absence of fixed prices for the items purchased, it was never certain how much they would receive with the goods available for payment. Still, those people were fairly content with whatever they got.

Today, a man sits in a luxurious car and drives to work. The workplace is also designed with all the facilities for the employees.

At the end of the month, a pre-determined amount is transferred to an individual's account to compensate for his/her services.

This has made budgeting much easier. Fulfilling one's needs does not require as much effort as it used to. There are so many extra luxuries and facilities that the previous generations couldn't even think about.

Despite the advancement in the overall standard of living, something seems amiss. The aforementioned feelings such as satisfaction and contentment are diminishing when they should be on the rise. Our life is being so much easier by science and technology each day, then why do we feel so uninspired?

It seems like we're drifting away from happiness. We're collectively destroying the elements that were responsible for making living things feel good. The question is, what are we doing so terribly, wrong?

To solve this riddle, we must understand the various aspects of human nature in more detail. Generally, when a person achieves something after a long and hard struggle, he/she values it more. A path filled with hardships makes the victory even sweeter.

But today, we have everything handed to us on a platter. The refrigerator is loaded with supplies, there are clean clothes to wear, and a comfortable home with all the necessary facilities. As a result, we have stopped valuing our blessings.

Moreover, the modern lifestyle has taken away some of the key factors of emotional stability. These include person-to-person interaction, natural environment, simple living, etc. So, we're not only becoming lazy and ungrateful but in a way, we're also digging our own grave.

This has been going on for the last few decades now. Thankfully, a small section of the world's population is finally realizing the damage being done. People are gradually waking up to the toxicity of the current lifestyle.

On one hand, we're becoming more distanced from each other as virtual connections overtake physical meetings. A trend that has been popularized even more by the occurrence of a pandemic. From work to social gatherings, everything is being done through online mediums.

On the other hand, this increased global outreach is also connecting us to previously unknown areas. We're learning more about different cultures and lifestyles. People living miles apart can relate to each other's problems and share solutions accordingly.

The few people in every part of the world who wish for a better lifestyle are encouraged when they hear similar voices from a different region. It feels good to have some validation and support for one's unique ideas. Like they say birds of a feather flock together, the like-minded people can learn from each other's experiences and work together towards the goal.

As mentioned earlier, the last few decades have been particularly disastrous in terms of lifestyle habits. In the name of greater comfort and ease, we've become used to some extremely unhealthy habits. In the form of poor mental and physical health, we're reaping what we've sowed ourselves.

For example, robots and machines are replacing human manpower. This has not only made human beings lazier but also decreased their mental and physical activities. In some cases, it has also resulted in unemployment and redundancies.

It may seem like a more feasible option to get work done mechanically, but that product/service will be missing the value provided by the human touch. Machines do not have the natural skills that enable human beings to excel at tasks. These skills include knowledge and understanding, problem-solving, sensitivity, etc.

Now imagine growing a plant under a bulb. It may seem like it is growing alright apparently, but comparing it with a plant grown under sunlight would reveal the true picture. Artificial lights obviously can't replace the energy provided by natural sunlight.

Of course, this view can be disputed by those who are devoted to the cause of science and technology. Some people want science to completely take over our lives. But the far-sighted ones have already realized the limitations of science and technology.

Being replaced by machines is just one example of the setbacks that humans have suffered lately. The current lifestyle has severely hampered the mental peace of most people. And when you feel miserable, there's not much that you can achieve in life.

So, the world is currently adapting to this situation. Efforts are being made to ensure that our upcoming generations do not suffer from the short-termism that we have exhibited. New and innovative ways of living are being experimented with, in different parts of the world.

Like we said, one advantage of this greater accessibility to the people living in other countries is that we can all learn from each other's lifestyles. One can seek inspiration and ideas from rural and urban areas alike. In the text below, let us learn a little more about the different new lifestyle trends being observed everywhere.

Europe

Europe may not cover a very large area, but it holds a significant influence over the world. It is considered the most developed one among all continents. Out of a total of 51 countries situated here, many are global leaders.

So understandably, this region has enjoyed a steady period of prosperity for most of recent history. Life has been comfortable and convenient. But have you ever witnessed something so good that it starts to seem boring?

We're not saying that European people have become tired of living comfortably. However, they're bothered by the monotony of the current lifestyle. They've realized that too much comfort does not always equate to an equal amount of happiness.

For example, if a team dominates a sports competition every year, the results start getting too predictable. And so much predictability ruins the fun of the game. Even winners feel less and less happy with each victory because the competition starts losing its charm.

To regain the lost 'charm' in life, Europe seems to be at the forefront. In other words, people are desperately looking for new activities and habits to break free from the current routine. The dissatisfaction is not due to poverty or deprivation but merely because of the emotional needs being ignored for too long.

The formation of the European Union proved to be a game-changer in this continent. The alliance brought great economic benefits for all the member countries. In terms of progress and development, the treaty put the region way ahead of the others.

Interestingly, the statistics regarding the mental health of people living in the EU are not as impressive. According to a report, more than 1 in 6 people across the EU countries suffer from mental health issues. That would mean about 84 million people a year in total.

This is probably why Europe is emerging as a hub of new lifestyle trends. These trends are focused on rejuvenating one's mind and body. It's quite encouraging to see that more and more people are now realizing the importance of prioritizing the needs of their minds and bodies.

Interestingly, for European people, the answer lies in their ancient ways. Old lifestyles are re-emerging due to their relevance in recent times. The trends being popularized today are just new and improved versions of the customs that have been followed for centuries.

The most significant reason for feeling unhappy these days is fatigue. Your mind, body, soul, every part of you is tired from the excessive work. So, the first step towards restoring happiness is to just relax.

Niksen

Niksen, the Dutch lifestyle teaches you to do just that. In this trend, you spend brief moments of idleness to cleanse your mind of unnecessary thoughts. For a few minutes, you just simply, 'let go'.

In her book titled "Niksen: The Power Of Doing Nothing", Tess Jansen repeatedly describes this lifestyle as 'simply doing nothing'. The book introduces you to several ways in which Niksen can be practiced. For example, just enjoying the warmth of your morning coffee with a blank mind.

Understanding this concept can be a little tricky for some people. This is because there is no clear description of how to live life the Niksen way. Moreover, one may wonder how can one adopt remaining idle as a regular habit?

Think of this as giving an overheated engine some rest so that it comes back to the normal temperature. The engine isn't doing anything during that rest period, but even then it is carrying out a much-needed activity to perform better later. It is also recuperating from the exhaustion it suffered earlier.

In Niksen, you have such rest periods regularly. You consciously do nothing for some time. You let your mind be vacant of all thoughts and just enjoy some minutes of peace.

The idea isn't to go to a secluded place to distance yourself from all that is happening around you. You can practice Niksen right in the midst of chaos by concentrating on yourself. It allows you to briefly detach yourself from the stress built up in your mind and body as well as external factors that cause worry.

So, how does this lifestyle ensure living a happier life? Firstly, it prevents you from burnout which is often the root cause of excessive stress and fatigue. It keeps you fresher and more energetic.

Secondly, these few moments to focus on yourself allow you to realize that prioritizing yourself is the key to happiness. If you're there for yourself, everything else can be dealt with. Your health and wellbeing matter the most and every other concern is secondary.

Jansen's book also compares Niksen with a slightly older, better-known trend of Hygge. Hygge is somewhat like a predecessor to Niksen. While both these lifestyle trends are slightly different in practice, the basic idea behind both is quite similar.

As explained in the text above, Niksen requires you to remain idle and relax. On the other hand, Hygge is about doing little things that help you relax. These are small, recreational activities that are meant to make you feel lighter.

The modes of relaxation vary from person to person. Some people like listening to music while others relax by reading a good book. Therefore, the Hygge lifestyle is just a flexible concept that allows you to enjoy your favorite activity.

But the crux remains the same, to give you a few moments of peace. Whatever you're doing should have your complete attention. All your senses should be engaged in the present moment instead of worrying about the future or lamenting the past.

For example, if you're curled up in a blanket and watching a tv show, there should be nothing else on your mind. You should be totally engrossed in the action on your tv screen. Anything you did earlier or are going to do later should become insignificant.

Hygge

There's a small detail that might make Hygge sound exclusive to colder regions. The lifestyle is focused on creating a warm and cozy environment. However, there is a deeper meaning to this concept.

The 'warmth' in the Hygge lifestyle is not just about heating the fireplace or having a bowl of hot soup. The warmth that we're talking about should penetrate your soul. It should melt the ice around your heart.

So, the essence of this lifestyle isn't increasing the indoor temperature. It's about filling your life with feelings of warmth and affection. Feelings that enhance the quality of your life.

For a better (and more detailed) explanation of this lifestyle, one may refer to Olivia Telford's Hygge: Discovering The Danish Art Of Happiness. The book elaborates how Denmark manages to top the list of happiest countries through the Hygge lifestyle. According to the author 'Hygge is meant to be felt and experienced, rather than defined'.

Friluftsliv

But what about the people who feel suffocated if they remain indoors for too long? Some people deem it necessary to get outdoors to feel fresh and happy. The appropriate solution for such people is the Friluftsliv lifestyle.

Friluftsliv means to be close to nature. Enjoying a beautiful sunset from your rooftop or going for a walk in a beautiful garden are examples of the Friluftsliv lifestyle. You absorb the goodness of the natural environment by being outdoors.

The idea is to have a rush of adrenaline by leaving this robotic lifestyle for some time. You could head to the mountains or have a picnic by the lake. Friluftsliv is all about feeling more alive and energetic by connecting to nature.

Since Friluftsliv is also a Scandinavian lifestyle, it sounds quite adventurous that the natives would want to spend time outside in the extreme cold. Some people may even argue that Hygge seems more appropriate for the climate. But to the followers of Friluftsliv, 'the weather isn't inappropriate, only the clothes are'.

Think of the reasons that you often cite for not wanting to go outside. Let's admit, the weather is often the main reason that stops us from experiencing nature. This is especially the case when we're feeling a little blue.

But by staying holed up in a closed space when all we need is some fresh air, we only make matters worse. Therefore, Friluftsliv makes such excuses irrelevant. It is like practically applying the concept of 'get up, dress up, and show up'.

The term Friluftsliv was introduced by a Norwegian poet and writer. To date, Norway remains the hub of this lifestyle. Some relevant information about experiencing this lifestyle in the mainland can be found here:

https://gettraveldealsnow.com/8-great-reasons-to-experience-friluftsliv-in-norway/

Coorie

Next up is the Coorie lifestyle which is quite similar to Friluftsliv. The Scottish word 'coorie' refers to snuggling or cozying up. 'Coorie in' is often a term that the adults of this area used to call children back indoors.

But as a lifestyle, the term differs a bit from its literal meaning. Coorie lifestyle involves striking a balance between your responsibilities and the simple pleasures in life. It leans more towards activities that allow you to relax out in the open.

Living life the Coorie way calls for a retreat from your day-to-day activities, preferably an outdoor one. Just like Frifluftsliv, Coorie emphasizes the importance of spending time in nature to attain happiness. However, the latter isn't so rigid in its meaning.

Examples of activities in the Coorie lifestyle include camping in the woods, gardening, fishing, etc. Instead of giving in to a monotonous routine, you try to have a break now and then. During this time, you completely switch off everything and try to unwind.

Lately, there has been a slight change in the way this lifestyle is observed. If you can't manage the time and resources to visit tourist spots, you can at least enjoy some leisure time at home. Creative activities like arts and crafts can also provide a similar joy that one experiences while being outdoors.

North America

North American continent consists of countries like Canada, the US, Mexico, Greenland, and many smaller island nations. Along with the indigenous population, the area is host to several other natives from all over the world. This is why its culture is a mix of several different beliefs and traditions.

So, it's a little trickier to define the lifestyle here. But one thing common across all these North American nations is their ahead-of-time planning. From Neil Armstrong being the first person to walk on the moon to Thomas Edison inventing the light bulb, Americans surely know how to pave the way to the future.

Since both these names belong to the US in particular, let us focus our discussion on the country. After all, it wouldn't be wrong to say that the country is like the face of the North American continent for most of the remaining parts of the world. Many US citizens in history have earned popularity by becoming trendsetters or predicting a future trend accurately.

Cocooning

A pioneer in this regard, Faith Popcorn had predicted Cocooning as a lifestyle trend in her book "The Popcorn Report" back in 1991. The author is known for her accuracy in forecasting future trends. In her words, cocooning is "the impulse to go inside when it just gets too tough and scary outside. To pull a shell of safety around yourself, so you're not at the mercy of a mean, unpredictable world - those harassments and assaults that run the gamut from rude waiters and noise pollution to crack-crime, recession, and AIDS. Cocooning is about insulation and avoidance, peace and protection, coziness and control-a sort of hyper-nesting."

In simpler words, cocooning is the urge to spend most of your time at home. It requires you to design your lifestyle and routine in a way that does not require regular outside visits. You only leave home it is necessary.

A more recent text about this lifestyle trend has explained this trend better for modern-day readers. According to Tess Jansen's Cocooning Lifestyle, "being able to stay inside the comfort of your home, in your bubble of happiness is nothing short of a luxury." This is how cocooning is presented as a way of happiness.

In 2013, a report prepared by a research agency called Wevolve for the European Forum on Forward-Looking Activities (EFFLA) outlined the lifestyle trends that would be prevalent in the US and Europe by the year 2020. The four main trends mentioned in the report were Augmented and Programmed Lives, Culture of Production and Sharing, Resilient and Proactive Citizens, and The Quest for Purpose (*Future lifestyles in Europe and in the United States in 2020*). Let us review this research in hindsight and compare the forecast trends with reality.

Augmented and Programmed Lives

The first lifestyle, "Augmented and Programmed Lives" foresaw the region being more digitally connected. It predicted significant developments in the field of science and technology. The research mentioned that areas such as health and diagnostics will improve while privacy and security will need greater attention.

Culture of Production and Sharing

The second lifestyle discussed in the report is "Culture of Production and Sharing". This section shed light on rising trends like DIY and abundant information. It also hinted at greater opportunities for customization.

Resilient and Proactive Citizens

"Resilient and Proactive Citizens", as the name suggests, referred to the upcoming changes in people's behaviors. It was predicted that there would be greater emphasis on principles like diversity. And the "communities and cities persist and thrive amid unforeseeable disruptions".

The Quest for Purpose

Lastly, "The Quest for Purpose" discussed the re-evaluation of life. It mentioned an increase in the focus on humanity and social issues. Contemplations like what is life all about.

Now, looking back at all these predictions, we can't help but marvel at the accuracy of the report. It's almost as if someone went to the future and then came back to make predictions. It is an accurate description of reality in 2020.

The question is, what do the current lifestyles say about the happiness levels in the region? Currently, United States ranks 18th in a list of happiest countries presented by Forbes (Bloom, 2020). Doesn't sound too bad, does it?

But then other qualitative indicators tell us a different story. For example, the US just witnessed serious political turmoil. Not only is this a rare occurrence for the country but it also indicates the level of frustration and dissatisfaction in people.

The neighbor country, Canada is far ahead on the happiness index. It ranks 11th and also enjoys a better reputation in terms of peace and equality lately. Needless to say, this reflects in the people's level of satisfaction as well.

So, the main takeaway from this continent's lifestyle, for those seeking happiness in life is that having a more empathetic approach towards people and the environment in general help. It increases contentment and also improves the overall quality of life for a society. Therefore, to feel truly happy ourselves, we have to start caring about our surroundings too.

Another thing to learn from this region is to ensure that citizens' rights are protected. Not doing so will result in unrest no matter how capable and in control your administration is. We saw this recently with movements like Black Lives Matter.

Lastly, giving people greater autonomy makes them feel happier as well. The DIY trend we talked about is just a small indication of this. If people feel like their lives are being monitored all the time or that their freedom is being compromised, they will be annoyed and frustrated at the disregard for privacy.

South America

South America has a vibrant culture throughout. Whether it is the street art in Sao Paulo, Brazil, or the Colombian cumbia, there is nothing subtle about it. The colors, attire, and music, everything is loud and vivacious.

Imagine yourself as a tourist visiting Argentina, witnessing tango being performed at the corner of a street in Buenos Aires. You would also feel like forgetting about everything else and just dancing your heart out. Life would seem quite enjoyable and pleasing at that moment.

In terms of geography, South America has a variety of features to offer. From mountains to river basins and coastal lands, there is enough natural beauty to mesmerize the natives and the tourists alike. You can gauge the area's diversity from the fact that the world's biggest rainforest the Amazon and the driest place, the Atacama Desert are both located here.

Unfortunately, most countries in South America still have significantly high poverty rates. This is probably why all these amazing land features have not been utilized to their full potential. Tourism, in many parts, still hasn't flourished as much as it should have.

However, the political aspects of this region are an entirely different debate. The 'happiness' for South American people comes from their day-to-day actions and not from the way that the state treats them. Their carefree nature lets them enjoy each moment despite several challenges faced by the economy.

A study published on IDB's website talks about the same disparity between the GDP and happiness levels of South American natives (Conci, 2019). It credits the pride taken in the cultural values for life satisfaction. The article also discusses the effects of having a strong system of emotional support on one's mental and psychological wellbeing.

So, this gives us the first lesson in happiness from this part of the world. Resilience is an ideal quality to have for anybody who wants to remain happy. Nobody can guarantee an absence of adversities in life but one can surely choose to be unperturbed by them.

Staying close to your loved ones can make you worry less about materialistic things. Communication with someone who understands you and loves you unconditionally can be therapeutic no matter how difficult the situation is. Having strong emotional connections helps in maintaining sound mental health.

For those who do not have a reliable social circle, remember the tourist watching the tango in the example we shared earlier? Just listening to the narration of this scene can make you feel lively and energetic. So, even if you don't have a permanent support system, surrounding yourself with people who want to enjoy life can ensure your happiness as well.

The South American culture evolved into what it is today with several different influences from time to time. At first, it was just the indigenous tribes and their traditions, then there was a wave of African influence followed by the customs introduced by Asian and European immigrants. Therefore, currently, the lifestyle has a flavor of each of these different cultures.

Another message that this evolution conveys is that instead of looking at new influences with contempt, we can pick and choose the best parts and incorporate them into our lives. This will only enhance the quality of our life. Just like adding new and fragrant flowers adds to the beauty of a bouquet.

Antarctica

It may feel absurd to see Antarctica being mentioned in a discussion regarding lifestyles. The area does not even have a permanent population, to begin with. But we simply couldn't rob the region of its status as a continent.

Going back in time, you might recall drawing igloos as a part of the Antarctic lifestyle. What seemed like a fun activity in childhood, has a more serious meaning when perceived as an adult. Those igloos were symbolic of a distinct lifestyle.

The shape of an igloo is quite similar to that of a turtle. The turtle also hides from perceived danger in its dome-shaped shell. In the case of igloos, humans hide from extreme cold and snow in the domed structure.

In a harsh environment, survival becomes the top priority of any living thing. Some warmth and protection from the subzero temperatures can make you feel better. Thus it wouldn't be wrong to say that feeling safe and secure is the first and foremost requirement to feel happier.

Antarctica is visited by a few thousand people every year. Sometimes teams are stationed there for several months. But apart from this, the continent does not people living there regularly.

So, anyone required to live there temporarily is not looking for a comfortable living or a luxurious life. It is only about surviving the harsh climate. Such experiences can teach us a lot about basic human instincts.

TO SUM IT UP, YOU CANNOT FEEL HAPPY IF YOU FEEL THREATENED OR UNSAFE.

IF YOU WISH TO LIVE A HAPPIER LIFE, YOU MUST LEARN TO GET RID OF ANYTHING THAT THREATENS YOUR MENTAL PEACE.

BEING MENTALLY AND PHYSICALLY AT EASE WILL IMPROVE YOUR MOOD GREATLY.

For this, you must choose your surroundings wisely. Any person or thing that ruins your happiness does not belong in your life. You must also learn to adjust to difficult situations temporarily as long as you keep your focus on the ultimate goal of achieving happiness.

Australia

It is often said that smaller units are easier to manage. Similarly, smaller continents tend to have lesser issues due to the presence of fewer countries. Luckily for Australia, this number is quite small.

It's not like a continent is one unit run by a single administration. But the lesser autonomous nations dwelling in an area, the lesser the chances of conflicts arising. Australia is sometimes referred to as Oceania to differentiate it from the largest country in the continent, which also goes by the same name i.e Australia.

There are several small islands on this continent. The lifestyles are quite similar due to the similarities in geographical features. But the most significant part remains the country of Australia, which also happens to be the sixth-largest country in the world (by area).

The Aussie Way of Life

The Australian lifestyle, or informally the Aussie way of living is quite casual. The nation enjoys popularity in many sports of the world, which shows that its energy is being channelized in the right manner. Notable contributions have been made in cricket, rugby, athletics, etc.

But that is not the only indicator of the country's youth indulging in healthy activities. The country has one of the highest life expectancy rates in the world. This can only be achieved if both your mental and physical health are well looked after.

Talking about healthcare, the country has a well-developed system in place. The same can be said about other necessities/facilities that a state owes to its citizens. Overall, the country truly lives up to its reputation of being one of the most developed nations in the world.

As a society, the Aussies have high regard for their values. These include equality, freedom, tolerance, compassion, etc. Let's get a more detailed view of the Aussie lifestyle through the following reports.

An article titled "A Handy Guide To the Australian Lifestyle" shared on australia.com would tell you all that you need to know as a potential tourist. It includes information about the attitude of the Australian people, cultural history, the love for food and joint celebrations, etc. But the most relevant part for you, if you're planning to visit the country, is that about outdoor life.

It is worth mentioning here that the Australian landscape varies drastically throughout the territory. From stunning coral reefs and beaches to snowy mountains, from rainforests to deserts, the country has it all. Therefore if you want to know more about the different geographical features, it is advised to take adequate time in planning your trip.

The outdoor life consists of fun activities like kayaking, bike rides, swimming, etc. Australians do not wait for a holiday period or a break from the work routine. They enjoy such recreational activities regularly.

A report by Commisceo Global lists all the salient features of the Aussie culture quite comprehensively. Mentioning the 'Aussie modesty' the report claims that the Australians lay strong emphasis on authenticity and humility. It also enlists some self-explanatory pieces of evidence of this humility.

For example, according to the report, Aussies do not like to brag about their achievements and also disapprove of someone else doing the same. They enjoy self-deprecatory humor which is impossible for arrogant people. Moreover, the Australians downplay their success 'to ensure they are not perceived as achievement-oriented.

Another commonly known habit of the countrymen is how they refer to each other as 'mates' in a friendly manner. Even the most widely used greeting in the country is 'g'day mate' (i.e good day, mate). Australians like to keep things informal and dislike pretense of any kind.

Lastly, since we mentioned Australian values before, it is important to share some more insights about the same. For this, let's refer to an opinion piece available on the website of ABC News. The article posted in 2017 is titled 'The 10 most Australian values that make Australia so valuable'.

The author enlists simple things like sitting at the front seat in a taxi and 'the gift of the nature strip' as part of the Aussie values. He expresses resentment at the act of hopping into the backseat when you hire a taxi, which is the norm in several other cultures. With 'gift of the nature strip' he explains that anything discarded by a household can be taken by a passerby without any question or explanation.

Understanding the motive behind these rather simple traditions fills you with respect for the culture. Being egalitarians, Australians do not want to humiliate or look down upon another human being. They want to treat everybody as their equal.

Understandably, all the residents would feel quite satisfied and happy with this kind of respect. There are lesser chances of injustice which automatically increases contentment. It also reduces the occurrence of street crimes such as theft and assault.

Due to its high regard for all these values, Australia is among the best-governed countries in the world. Hence, other regions can surely learn from its example to ensure a happier population. Focusing on justice and equality can help resolve several social issues prevailing in different parts of the world.

Africa

A few years ago, an image of a Nigerian child with a female aid worker went viral. In that picture, there was a 2-year-old boy abandoned for being a 'witch'. The aid worker was helping the kid drink water from the bottle she was holding.

Through this picture, the world got to know about an extremely toxic trend that is prevalent in this part of the world. The abandoned child was in extremely poor health and his condition sensitized the world about the issue. After that, there was an immense outpouring of support from all over the world for the cause of saving such children and giving them a better future.

Through social media, we often learn about customs prevailing in other parts of the world that we're completely oblivious to. We realize how limited our knowledge is and how disconnected we are from the rest of humanity. Exchanging pleasantries on social media is much easier than working to improve the condition of the less fortunate population of the world.

The purpose of starting this discussion with this example is not to demean a certain group of people. It is just to drive the attention away from the comfortable lifestyles that we have discussed earlier. Once in a while, all of us need such eyeopeners.

It would be unfair to compare the African lifestyle with other continents that are years and years ahead of it in terms of development. But as we've seen in other regions as well, a poor economic condition does not necessarily mean poor happiness levels as well. People can choose to be happy despite all their difficulties.

However, in Africa, the inconveniences people face daily are far from minor. For a visitor from a developed country, life here would seem quite unbearable. Afflicted by extreme poverty, the natives do not even have access to the basic necessities of life.

Housing is mostly informal and there is no proper infrastructure. Facilities such as sanitation and the supply of clean water are almost nonexistent. In short, discussing the African lifestyle almost makes you feel guilty for expecting some happiness tips from the region.

But in the spirit of salvaging what we can, let's focus on the cultural aspects of this area. And the African culture doesn't disappoint in any way. From colorful clothing to the music of drumbeats, it is as vibrant as it can be.

Just like a person on his/her deathbed knows the value of time better than anybody else, it seems like people in adversity realize the importance of happiness more than those living comfortably. Despite all the difficulties that the African natives face, they don't miss a chance to enjoy life. You can see their zest reflecting in arts and craft, cuisine, attire, folklore, and all the day-to-day affairs.

If someone simply tells you to be happy in all situations, it may sound like a piece of hollow advice. But when you see people leading by example, it inspires you a great deal. In terms of happiness, there's a lot that one can learn from the less privileged areas.

Asia

To denote a stark contrast between two things, we often term them as being as different as east and west. Usually, the simile is used to emphasize the differences between the continents in the eastern and western hemispheres. But with Asia, this could even mean the difference between the eastern and western parts of the same continent.

Asia is the largest one among all seven continents. Not only does it cover the largest area but also has the highest population. Moreover, it encompasses several different nations with completely different lifestyles, making it seem like a whole world on its own.

Therefore it is a little difficult to do justice to all the cultures in one go. Each ethnic group dwelling on the continent has an elaborate history and set of traditions. For a brief overview of the prominent lifestyles, the continent can be divided into five subregions to make it easier to discuss the different cultures.

These are namely Central Asia, East Asia, South Asia, Southeast Asia, and Western Asia. Each of these parts has a prominent global presence because of the geographical location and impact on the political dynamics. Asia is also the fastest-growing continent in terms of economy.

Starting with Central Asia, we have countries like Kazakhstan, Kyrgyzstan, Turkmenistan, Tajikistan, and Uzbekistan in this region. All these nations were formerly part of the USSR. The current culture in Central Asia is an amalgamation of Middle Eastern values and Russian influence.

The Central Asian people mostly belong to the Muslim faith. The landscape in this region is dominated by steppes (a landform that typically includes unforested grasslands), and deserts. The climate is generally dry with very low levels of precipitation.

The area was occupied by the Chinese, the Turks, the Mongols, and the Russians during different eras. So, the culture includes customs and traditions from different ethnic groups. The region did not have a distinct identity before the 1990s and hence, its culture isn't too well documented.

Overall, the lifestyle here is simple and conservative. Central Asian people are warm and hospitable. As these nations have gained independence rather recently, they are still on their way to establish a mark on the global landscape.

The happiness levels in Central Asia aren't too impressive. Repeated occupations and conquests have probably led to people feeling discontent. The good news is, these countries are finally free to find their happiness.

So, for now, we can safely say that unfair treatment does not go down well with any people. Sooner or later, it results in the decay of the entire society. If we stand for a happier world, it automatically means that we stand against injustice and illegal occupations.

Moving on to East Asia is almost like stepping into a different planet. With the presence of superpowers like China and Japan, the region is on another level of development. If statistics are to be believed, the region would surpass the western economies in the upcoming years.

Prominent East Asian countries such as China, Japan, South Korea, and Taiwan are all highly developed. It wouldn't be wrong to say that if any region in Asia has the resources to experiment with innovative lifestyles, it is East Asia. Of course, there are smaller countries that are still struggling, but let's see what can we learn about happiness from this part of the world.

Mottainai

The most relevant, modern lifestyle trend to emerge from Eastern Asia (or Asia in general) is Mottainai. The Japanese word is an exclamation that can be translated to 'what a waste!'. In other words, the term is used to express regret over wasting something.

As a lifestyle, the concept of Mottainai is to use your resources more carefully. Instead of being wasteful, you recycle and reuse whatever you can. While environmentalists often use the 3 R's to explain an eco-friendly lifestyle i.e Reduce, Recycle and Reuse, Mottainai also adds a fourth R, which denotes Respect, to this list.

This means that you show respect for all the things that you use. When you start respecting and valuing things, you would not throw them away carelessly. The concept finds its origin in the Buddhist belief that everything has a spirit and must be treated kindly.

The idea of not being wasteful extends to food, clothes, or any product that you use. When you incorporate this thinking into your lifestyle, you would automatically start thinking of innovative ways to reduce wastage. The first step is to start perceiving life and everything it contains as an incredible gift that must be cherished.

What this does to us is that it grounds us and instills humility in our personality. You care more about objects, the environment, and other people as well. So, this virtuous conduct helps in increasing contentment and inner peace.

South Asia consists of countries like India, Pakistan, Bangladesh, Sri Lanka, Afghanistan, Nepal, Bhutan, and the Maldives. Most of this area was under the reign of Mughal Emperors for a very long time. Their lavish lifestyle is still criticized for wasting valuable resources which could have been a gamechanger for this area.

History is marred with wars, political instability, and many social issues. India, Pakistan, and Bangladesh were jointly known as the subcontinent in the past. The area had to fight its way to independence from the British Raj and subsequently from each other.

Afghanistan is still reeling from the effects of war. It is one of the unhappiest places in the world. The remaining nations are not doing much better either.

But the area has no shortage of natural resources. In most parts, people depend on agriculture and livestock for a living. South Asia is blessed with a variety of beautiful land features.

Although the growth of the science and technology sector has picked up speed lately, the region still has a long way to go in terms of development. The happiest South Asian country is Pakistan (ranked 66th in the world), followed by Maldives (87th in the world) and Nepal (92nd in the world) (Sheikh, 2020).

Although these numbers aren't great, they seem like a miracle when you look at the challenges these countries have faced. High rates of poverty, terrorism and bloodshed, natural disasters, and whatnot. Yet the people remain jovial and enthusiastic instead of complaining about their problems.

South Asians take great pride in their heritage and history. They're extremely proud of their ancestors who fought for their freedom. Patriotism and remembering the sacrifices of their forefathers make them remain grateful no matter how difficult the situation gets.

In Southeast Asia, there are both mainlands and island nations. So it's a mix of inland and coastal areas. Better known countries from this region are Indonesia, Malaysia, Thailand, Singapore, Philippines, etc.

Due to its unique location and scenic beauty, the region is quite famous among international tourists. Visitors can experience the exotic beach life or enjoy the unique architecture. The region offers a variety of equally tempting choices.

Lately, there have been a lot of complaints about environmental damage. The area has faced severe issues because of human negligence. Along with urbanization and deforestation, carelessness exhibited by the visiting tourists is also one of the main causes of these environmental issues.

So, we need to understand that if we derive enjoyment from something, we must also learn to value it. Exploitation will only result in our happiness vanishing sooner than we would realize. We can't destroy the reasons for happiness and then sit and complain about it.

Endangered species, water security issues, pollution are all examples of problems that we have created ourselves. Today, these issues are causing great distress. Hence, to live more happily, we should pay greater attention to our environment and its constituents.

Lastly, the region of Western Asia is dominated by the Arab peninsula. The area is often grouped in the Middle East along with Egypt and Turkey. But the main influence on the overall culture remains that of the Arab countries including Saudi Arabia, UAE, Bahrain, Oman, Kuwait, etc.

The Arabs are known for their extravagance and lavish lifestyle. The oil-rich nations enjoy a fairly high standard of living. For the sake of this discussion, let's assume these countries are representative of Western Asia in general.

The Arab countries do considerably well in happiness rankings. Whether this has something to do with the area's wealth remains unclear. But there are other traits that we can attribute this happiness to.

For example, the Arabs like mingling with others instead of enjoying some private time. They like to live with honor and dignity. They're also well known for their generosity.

Suggesting that adhering to these values may help you live happier sounds rather simple, doesn't it? Well, not in recent times. These days it is quite difficult to stick to such beliefs.

Overall, one must try to strike a balance between fulfilling material needs and developing a sound character. Over-reliance on either can make you feel incomplete. You must also keep in mind that your concepts would keep evolving with age and this will be an unending process.

Global lifestyles: an overview

From the above discussion, we can conclude that there is something to learn from every culture. There is something good in every situation which we fail to acknowledge when we become too one-dimensional. In short, life would not always be a bed of roses and that should not be a reason for your unhappiness.

Although the salient features of each continent would have given you some idea about the different cultures prevailing in the world, this list is far from comprehensive. The truth is, it is almost impossible to cover all the aspects of so many lifestyles in a single text. Even discussing the different ethnicities dwelling within a country in complete detail would require a longer discussion than we have done to cover the entire world.

The idea is to use this information as a starting point and conducting your in-depth analysis. You don't need to adopt one lifestyle in its entirety. You can choose the best parts about each one and create your way of living a more comfortable life.

The more you explore the world, the greater ideas you will have for a happier living. Luckily these days you don't even have to travel to learn about different cultures. All the information you may need is just a click away on the internet.

Our purpose is to open your eyes to newer possibilities. When you learn more about the world your problems and worries start to seem small and insignificant. If you feel compelled to apply any of the things you have learned about the other parts of the world, you're already one step closer to happiness.

Life after COVID-19

The world is facing a unique crisis right now. The struggle to stay safe and protected has almost become a lifestyle. The past year has brought many changes to our lives and the trend is likely to continue for the next few months as well.

Although this is a once-in-a-lifetime situation, it does not necessarily have to be spent as a punishment. Humanity is fighting a war against a common enemy which requires us to stay strong and optimistic. This battle is more tiresome for the nerves as compared to the physical abilities.

Luckily, several trends that we have mentioned in the text above also coincide with the current situation. The intermittent lockdowns all over the world call for out-of-the-box solutions, just like the ones we have presented in the text above.

Hygge is all about cozying up at home. Cocooning requires you to stay at home most of the time. Niksen is enjoying idleness for some time.

In one way or the other, this is all that we have been doing. Staying at home to protect ourselves and trying to make the most of this time. It's almost like the universe is giving us a message about fixing our lifestyles.

Another lesson that this whole situation has taught us is that if we start sharing information, we would be much better equipped to face our challenges. It is rightly said that two heads are better than one. If we can combine our thinking skills create greater unity between nations, life would become much easier.

Not to turn this into a political debate but look at what is happening around us. It is like a rat race where the less fortunate nations are at the mercy of the superpowers. While we may not have the power to change the global dynamics, we can at least do things differently in our individual lives.

The last year has been quite traumatic for everybody. Some suffered healthwise, some lost their loved ones and some faced losses at work. In one way or the other, everyone has suffered personal setbacks.

Besides that, seeing so many tragedies in the world has been a nightmarish experience. So, undoubtedly, we need to take the necessary steps to heal and recover from all these events. We also need to change ourselves and utilize the important life lessons that this time has taught us. Let's look at some things that we need to keep in mind moving forward.

Reset your priorities

This has also been a time of some much-needed realizations. People have realized that they were focusing too much on a single aspect and neglecting everything else in life. Some have decided to spend more time with family while others have resolved to travel more. In any case, make sure that your priorities are aligned with your happiness and not any external pressure.

Take frequent breaks

Life almost came to a standstill everywhere for some time. But that break was temporary and necessary to protect everyone's health and wellbeing. Impatience would have proved deadly at that time (and unfortunately it did, for some people). So, whenever you feel like things are getting too overwhelming, just disconnect from everything and take some time to unwind.

Seek help

Our pride often stops us from showing our vulnerable side. Many people are quite uncomfortable admitting that they're struggling with their emotions. COVID-19 and the related issues were a once-in-a-lifetime kind of event. So, make sure you share your feelings with a loved one or seek professional help if needed.

Be considerate

During this pandemic, it didn't feel right to celebrate a personal gain when the world was suffering so much. In the future, we must remember that our celebrations should not hurt the sentiments of the less privileged ones. Instead of wasting resources and being extravagant, we should try to use our privilege to help others.

Look after yourself

If you slept well, took out time for self-care, read a book, or did something you like which felt like an accomplishment, think again. All these things should be a regular part of your routine and not done because a lockdown gave you a lot of spare time. Whether it is 5 minutes or 1 hour, there should be some time dedicated to your wellbeing every day.

CHAPTER 3
WHAT DETERMINES YOUR LIFESTYLE?

Getting a box of chocolates is a great feeling. But if it is an assorted box with each piece carefully selected according to your choice, it becomes even more priceless. The word 'customized' automatically makes something a lot more special.

In most workplaces, there is an automatic system in place to check-in to work every day. For example, employees need to mark their attendance with a biometric fingerprint or face recognition. This is done to ensure that the attendance is marked in a hassle-free manner and to record the time when the employee arrived at work.

Similar checks are in place to note the check-out timings. Such tools are used for performance evaluation and sometimes even directly linked to the calculation of daily wages. The hours worked are carefully monitored and affect the individual's prospects.

This is just one of the examples of the kind of rules imposed to assess your performance. Luckily, the universe has not made any strict rules regarding living. We're free to choose the lifestyle we want.

To describe it poetically, it has given us a blank canvas to paint whatever kind of picture we want. We can use our favorite colors and styles. In the aforementioned example of chocolate boxes, life can be a 'customized' assorted one if we want.

But sometimes, when things are not too well-defined, it may seem confusing to choose the right way. In this case, you may be wondering how to choose which daily habits are best for you. Here are some considerations that would make this decision easier for you.

Goals

What are the targets that you want to achieve in life? Do you want fame and wealth or you want to quietly help the needy? At what age do you plan to retire?

These are some of the questions that you'll be asking yourself when deciding your lifestyle. Some people believe in making strong, short-term plans and focusing on those. They believe that if the immediate future is taken care of, long-term success would follow automatically.

Another view is that you should plan for the next 10 to 20 years and dedicate all your energies towards those long-term goals. These may include a house at your favorite location, starting your own business, traveling the world, etc. This requires greater patience as you would give up temporary pleasures to focus on the long-term plans.

So, what we mean to say is that to know which day-to-day habits are best for you, you need to first decide what you want to achieve with those habits. It's just like knowing your destination before you choose a path. Taking the wrong turn would only take you farther from your destination.

When you step into adulthood after the carefree teenage years, it takes some time to figure out your purpose. It is suggested to not rush during this phase. If you're still trying to decide your ultimate goal in life, there's nothing wrong with taking your time.

But once you decide what you want from life and chalk out the strategy for the same, you must develop a no-quit attitude. You must stick with the routine that you have chosen until you succeed in achieving your goals. You should not let difficulties make you aim lower.

Responsibilities

Having a lot of responsibilities can change your approach to life. It reduces choosing anything that involves a high degree of risk. People with dependent family members are less likely to make impulsive decisions.

If a person has to pay children's school fees, house rent, pay for the family's healthcare, etc, he/she would like to have a fixed earning per month. This would make budgeting easier and reduce stress. Since the pressure of responsibilities is already quite overwhelming, nobody would want to add to the uncertainty by opting for an unreliable job.

So, such a person would prefer a modest income with regular payments instead of a high-paying opportunity with a dubious future. Fulfilling the obligations would be the top priority. Any additional perks would just be a bonus.

On the other hand, if you're only responsible for yourself, you have the liberty to choose whatever you want. You may choose a high risk and high reward approach or even work infrequently if your needs are fulfilled. You wouldn't have to worry too much about a steady stream of income.

For greater mental peace, try to ascertain which one of these categories do you belong to. Then align your decision-making skills and daily habits with your situation. This would help you choose the most suitable habits according to your needs.

Nature of work

Some professions do not allow you to follow a strict routine. For example, a doctor, a policeman, or a firefighter can be called to work whenever a need arises. In emergencies, such professionals are required to work additional hours as well.

Apart from this, other factors influence your routine. For instance, if you work with international clients, you need to keep your working hours flexible to ensure effective communication. Or, if you work with a security agency, you need to stay vigilant all the time.

In such cases, the rules that apply to 9 to 5 jobs would not apply to you. The lifestyle suggestions made with these regular employees in mind would not cater to those who work odd hours. So, you need to carefully study different lifestyles before you settle for the right one.

Personality

Introverts would like lifestyles that involve staying in while extroverts would look for more outdoor activities. Similarly, avid readers would want to have a library constructed at home and cinema-goers would prefer a theatre experience. These are purely personal choices and there's no right or wrong way to live.

So, the suitability of a lifestyle for you depends on all such factors. Your likes and dislikes play an important role in determining the right set of habits for you. The closer you stay to your basic nature, the happier you tend to feel.

When you forcefully do something against your nature, it makes you feel quite uncomfortable. Going for a swim if you don't like water would not make you happy no matter how many people tell you otherwise. Rely on your knowledge about your personality to decide what is best for you.

You should never give up your comfort to please other people. Choose the lifestyle that fits your personality. There must not be any pressure to adhere to social norms when it comes to personal habits.

Living conditions

Earlier, we spoke about cozy lifestyles like Hygge and Cocooning. But to a person living in a scorching desert, coziness would not be a relative consideration. The mere mention of something warm would cause great discomfort.

Similarly, the size or structure of your apartment/home, weather conditions, sunlight duration, etc affect your lifestyle choice. Your daily habits also depend on your area and the people you live with. Sometimes there are norms that people follow religiously and would not give them up at any cost.

Set of beliefs

This brings us to another important consideration i.e an individual's set of beliefs. It is important to mention that sometimes a certain idea may be against your religion, faith, or philosophy of life. This is why we have emphasized time and again that you can be flexible in your choices of daily habits.

For example, some faiths are already strictly against eating meat. Telling the followers of such a faith that leaving meat would make them happier would be quite futile. They could teach a thing or two about the benefits of not eating meat themselves.

General guidelines do not apply to specific situations. Happiness does not require you to compromise on your principles. That would be quite an insensitive suggestion to make.

Instead, you need to find your own comfortable and happy way of life. Just like finding your rhythm to the music playing in a certain club. In short, there is no 'one size fits all' way of life so you can always mold the ideas according to your needs.

Strength of willpower

A person tasked with something outside his/her comfort zone but having strong willpower will succeed in doing it nonetheless. He/she will somehow find the motivation to overcome the hesitation. Strong willpower makes tackling risks and challenges a little easier.

On the other hand, an individual who lacks will or intent will always find an excuse to give up. The task would seem too overwhelming and daunting if willpower is weak. It almost equates to giving up even before the battle has begun.

In short, strong willpower can make you move mountains while weak willpower will make a minor fever seem like a life-threatening disease. Therefore, before you set certain habits for yourself, you need to ask yourself whether you're mentally prepared to adhere to them. Or, whether you're willing to work on your willpower or not.

This isn't even a trait that can't be enhanced or changed. You can always strengthen your willpower by training yourself accordingly. What you need is the presence of a strong wish to achieve your goals.

Learning never stops

Once we reach adulthood, we become a little reluctant to learn new things. We start thinking that we already know enough to live our remaining life comfortably. Mostly, we also become quite rigid in our opinions.

But the fact is that no matter how old or experienced we are, there is always room for more knowledge and improvement. The evolution process never stops until we're dead. So, we needn't be so averse to newer concepts.

Instead of fearing change, we need to embrace it wholeheartedly. You may have often heard that 'change is the only constant'. Hence, why not get used to something that we are bound to encounter again and again in our lives.

A few decades ago, nobody could have known the use of touchscreen gadgets. Today, even a little child can use these quite efficiently. And aren't we all grateful for the ease this has brought into our lives?

In an earlier chapter, we discussed how human ways evolved. We mentioned life in caves and compared it to the comfortable living today. Had those cavemen restricted change, we wouldn't have been where we are today.

In every era, there are naysayers as well as brave people who are willing to try newer, better alternatives. Those brave people end up changing the destiny of humankind from time to time. Now, it is upon us to decide which group do we wish to associate ourselves with.

Even today, if you look around yourself, you will find examples of both these kinds. For example, when COVID-19 struck, the world was divided in its opinions. There were all kinds of conspiracy theories circulating in different parts of the work.

Now, when different pharmaceutical companies have developed a vaccine, conspiracy theorists are quite active again. Some people want to give it a chance and encourage others as well. At the same time, some people are strongly opposing the idea and want others to refrain from it as well.

Seeing how much the world has suffered recently, the latter group seems a bit irrational. When you stand against change, you also stand against hope, in a way. You block the path to progress further in life.

Therefore, you never know which single change will transform your entire life. Being apprehensive before trying something new is quite natural. But this shouldn't be a reason to give up growth opportunities.

The reason we're emphasizing the need to evolve is that this reluctance to change often becomes the cause of our unhappiness. Even though we're discontent, we're just too scared to live differently. To change how we feel, we must learn to let go of our inhibitions.

Until then, even if somebody tells you about a million different lifestyles or gives you hundreds of inspirational ideas, it'll all be quite useless. The motivation to change whatever makes you unhappy has to come from within you. Nobody will be as affected by your feelings as you, so it's better to take matters into your own hands.

CHAPTER 4
SOME HABITS TO INCREASE HAPPINESS

In the previous chapters, we have tried to highlight various lifestyle trends from all over the world. But that is just one-half of the objective behind this text. The other equally important half is to present ideas for greater happiness in life.

You never attain unending happiness from a single act. For example, if completing a degree gives you immense happiness, you can't dwell on that feeling forever. After a point, the degree would start to seem like a useless piece of paper if it doesn't add value to your life.

Now consider getting employed by a prestigious company based on that degree. You would reap the benefits of that degree regularly. Thus, all the hard work behind it would seem more meaningful and worthwhile.

Achievements tend to lose their charm if they're not acknowledged by others. And people would not appreciate your success if they don't see a positive change it has brought to your life. Sometimes, even if they do see you living a successful life, they do not give you the due credit because of vices like jealousy and hatred.

We're all familiar with Jim Carrey's famous quote about life in which he said:

> *"I think everybody should get rich and famous and do everything they ever dreamed of so they can see that it's not the answer."*

Fame, wealth, and all such non-spiritual pleasures come with an expiry date. Their pursuit is an exhausting experience for the soul. Once you reach your destination, you feel clueless about the way forward.

On the other hand, having happiness as your main objective keeps you grounded. You don't run after material gains but try things that you're passionate about. So the satisfaction you gain is more long-lasting.

Let's try to compare these two lifestyles through an example. The first one is like reaping a bumper crop and feeling like you're on top of the world. You sell it in the market and earn a fortune.

Now, becoming rich overnight is an enticing idea. You purchase everything that you had been dreaming of and feel like the luckiest man alive. But gradually, your earnings start depleting and you're worried about maintaining the same lifestyle in the future.

This would not have happened if you didn't become used to living luxuriously. Moreover, while you enjoyed the success of your last achievement, you did nothing to make sure it lasts.

Meanwhile, the second lifestyle is like sowing a tree and then nurturing it into a big, fruitful tree. You water it, protect the young plant from extreme weather and birds, and take care of it every day. Throughout that time, your only concern is that the plant grows well and becomes a healthy tree.

Even though you do not have a selfish motive, the flourishment of the plant gives you immense happiness. Each new leaf that grows, each new branch extended by the tree fills you with pure joy. You feel that your hard work is finally paying off.

Then, the tree starts returning the favor. It provides shade, is visually pleasing, and also bears fruit. This gain might seem much smaller than the previous example but it feels a lot more rewarding.

Moreover, the tree won't only benefit you for one or two seasons. The earning from it might be small but it is more reliable and sustainable. Hence, it guarantees greater satisfaction and lesser stress.

The moral of the story is that we need to lower our expectations to feel more content. At the same time, we have to constantly work on ourselves if we want to be happy in the long run. We must wake up each day and think of ways to make better use of our time.

Therefore, we can conclude that happiness can be achieved systematically by adopting the right daily habits. Some characteristics are particularly associated with happier living. Let us have a look at some of these habits.

Exercise

We all know the importance of exercise for physical fitness. But not as many people know the significance of staying active to maintain better mental health. Staying active is suggested as an effective way to feel better mentally and emotionally.

Exercise does not have to be a rigorous routine at the gym. You can go for a nice walk whenever you find some free time in the day. However, setting a fixed time for your daily stroll is recommended as it helps develop a habit.

If you can't manage the time to go for a walk, you can do some light exercises for short intervals during work. Stretching, yoga poses, and skipping rope are examples of some exercises that do not require a lot of equipment. If you're at home, you can also try fun activities like aerobics or dancing.

According to an article published in The New York Times, there is a beneficial relationship between being physically active and being happy. Citing research carried out by researchers at the University of Michigan, the report states that exercise can lower the risk of a person developing depression or anxiety. The type of exercise needed to improve happiness levels isn't specified and can depend on your personal preference.

In a previous chapter, we mentioned how the ancient people had better emotional health despite having an extremely tough lifestyle. After reading this research, one wonders if the taxing physical activities contributed to a greater level of happiness in those times.

People slept quite peacefully and had lesser health issues. This can be attributed to the physically strenuous tasks they carried out all day long. There was no concept of anti-depressants or sleeping pills and people still managed to remain calm.

Even today, after a tiring day, you fall asleep almost immediately as your head hits the pillow. No matter how sore your muscles are, the fatigue doesn't let you lay in the bed with your eyes wide open and think about every stressful thing in the world. So, you don't just feel fitter and more relaxed, but also sleep better which is another effective way to boost your mood.

Spend time with nature

The bigger a tree becomes, the deeper and stronger its roots become. Its 'growth' does not make it less connected to the soil that nourished it. The roots keep expanding and play an important role in holding the tree in its place.

For human beings, these 'roots' can mean several things. For example, the family that one was born and brought up in. The city that a person lived in while growing up. The ethnicity, the set of beliefs, the identity, etc.

But these are individual factors that would be different for everybody. We are looking for similar roots that make you feel part of a bigger community. Just like different trees that grow in the same soil.

When you suggest stargazing to someone who is not used to spending time under the open sky, the idea seems quite ordinary. But if you've ever witnessed a shooting star while observing the night sky, you would know what kind of amazing opportunities await nature lovers. There are always so many surprises to unveil.

Another example is feeling mesmerized every time you see a firefly. No artificial light can give you the same experience. Even the latest innovations in technology fail to affect you in the same way.

The reason is that nature's wonders induce an emotional response. Those little miracles cannot be recreated by humans or machines. The happiness of witnessing the universe's magic stays with you forever.

On the other hand, the emotions involved in scientific inventions and discoveries fade away as we become used to them. They surely make us happier, but only for making our lives better and easier. Not for the awe-inspiring reasons associated with natural elements.

Smile a lot

Nowadays, if someone smiles too much, he/she is termed delusional. In offices, at bus stops, or in all public places in general, we mostly get to see frowning or overly serious faces. Coming across a smiling face is a rarity and instead of finding it pleasantly surprising, we mostly find it quite weird.

A smile is not just an expression of happiness. It has a calming effect on a person's mind and body. An ever-smiling face does not indicate the absence of problems in your life but it shows how strong and well prepared you are to deal with those problems.

In a tense situation, when somebody smiles at you, you suddenly feel a lot better. The gesture seems more reassuring than any spoken word ever would. Not only does it soothe others but also calms your nerves.

Although this is not a foolproof solution for your problems, it helps keep you cool. According to a study published in Psychological Bulletin, your facial expressions do have a small effect on your feelings (Preidt, 2019). So, if you can feel even slightly better just by being more careful about your facial expressions, the idea is worth a shot.

Stay productive

Don't get us wrong, this isn't some kind of a strict order to get up and start working immediately. This is an encouragement to not give up and keep going no matter how little you're able to achieve.

What we're saying is something along the lines of Martin Luther King Jr's words about continuing to move forward. For those who are unaware of the quote, here is what the great man had said:

> *"If you can't fly then run, if you can't run then walk, if you can't walk then crawl, but whatever you do you have to keep moving forward."*
>
> *~ Martin Luther King Jr*

Productivity is not uniform on all days. It varies according to your mood, how you're feeling healthwise, other people's behavior towards you, the resources available on a particular day, etc. So, we're not saying that you should complete a certain amount of work regardless of all these factors.

This is the mistake that most of us make in recent times. We set productivity goals and achieving them becomes a matter of life and death. We start deriving our self-worth from the ability to achieve these goals.

Not only should our goals be achievable, but there should be considerations for the days when we don't feel like ourselves. And on those difficult days, we need to be a little kinder to ourselves. Every little task that we're able to accomplish should be appreciated.

The world is changing. To adjust our lives to the current situation, we must also make room for the deteriorating mental health of the overall population. Lack of productivity because of stress should never be a reason to shame the employees.

This is also because when people feel they're not being as productive as their usual selves, it discourages them from doing anything at all. They feel insufficient and the morale goes down significantly. Consequently, there's even more stress and anxiety.

Since an increasing number of people are also becoming self-employed recently, they can keep this habit in check. It is now easier to keep the schedule flexible and work according to your conditions. Therefore, the stress of not being equally productive every day should also decrease.

Eat healthy food

It may sound surprising to some people that some foods are more likely to increase stress, anxiety, and depression. The kind of food you consume has a direct effect on your overall health. It affects your mind, body, and emotions as well.

Some food items are also associated with lengthening or shortening the human lifespan. For example, red meat and tobacco reduce your potential lifespan while certain fruits, vegetables, and herbs help add a few years to life. The interesting thing is, the foods linked to decreasing the lifespan also hurt your mental health.

At the same time, the foods that help you live longer are also known to help in keeping you happier. This may not be a mere coincidence. Apart from scientific reasons like a fast metabolism and other health benefits, there may be another logical explanation for this.

What we mean to say is, that it is a well-known fact that a person who stays sad or depressed is more prone to illnesses. Your willpower is reduced and you have less strength to fight back. In this situation, if your immune system has already been weakened by eating unhealthy foods, it may lead to severe consequences.

Then some mood-boosting foods instantly make you feel better. These may vary from person to person based on personal choices.

However, some generally accepted examples of such food items are chocolates, nuts, and coffee.

Of course, these aren't like any magic potion that would eliminate all your sorrows at once. But this is where we get the idea of 'comfort food' from. When you're sad or upset, eating your favorite food can put you in a better mood.

When you're following a strict diet to achieve your goal weight, you often give up many of your favorite food items. This way, you may achieve the desired weight faster but the journey would seem boring and tiresome. An overly rigid approach would make a healthy habit seem like a punishment.

The idea is to be a little more flexible and also consider your emotional health while planning your diet. Enjoying a 'cheat meal' once in a while doesn't hurt. As long as you're not eating anything severely detrimental to your health, it is completely okay to enjoy a lavish meal with the sole objective of feeling happy.

Socialize

Discussing social life in the modern era can be a little confusing. We're a lot more connected due to the latest technology but a lot more disconnected emotionally. The emergence of social media seems to have caused as much damage as it has done well.

Most friendships that we're able to maintain throughout life are the ones that were developed early on in life. For some reason, we lose our ability to build strong social connections as we grow older. The friendships birthed in adulthood are mostly artificial or coincidental.

When you spend years and years being friends with somebody, you go through many conflicts as well. Of course, the love keeps growing with time but each confrontation also leaves a sour taste. As years go by, you also have to make peace with a lot of differences that arise between friends.

While this makes old friendships more durable, there is a unique charm in new friendships as well. It feels like a fresh start to life when two individuals share their views on the topics of mutual interest. You embark on a new journey that requires you to explore a lot of previously undiscovered paths.

Making new friends introduces you to newer perspectives. If new friends belong to a different area, religion, race, etc it diversifies your knowledge and thinking even more. Unfortunately, instead of using this as an opportunity to feel happier, we have limited ourselves to only befriending people that society approves of.

Restricting ourselves from reaching out to more people, for whatever reason, impacts our emotional health negatively. So, don't listen to anybody who stops you from interacting with a certain group of people. Just keep in mind that every new person you meet deserves to see the best version of you and remember you fondly.

Adequate sleep

Setting big goals that make you spend sleepless nights is a great thing. Aiming higher naturally gives you a reason to push yourself to work harder. But along with that, you also have to ensure that your mind and body can endure the extra workload.

Not getting enough sleep would make you feel tired most of the time. You will not have the motivation to do anything. In the long run, not getting enough sleep has severe detrimental effects on your physical and mental health.

Remember, this isn't a challenge to sleep as much you can to feel happier. Excessive sleep will also result in unexplained fatigue and health issues. The emphasis is on getting moderate sleep every day, not too little or too much.

Most experts put this at 7 to 9 hours a day. It is reported that not sleeping enough makes your brain's emotional centers 'run amok'. There is evidence regarding a lack of sleep, inducing negative thoughts in people.

Another important factor linked to happiness is the quality of sleep you get. Other than duration, the timing of your sleep also affects your mood. Sleeping earlier at night is preferable as compared to getting an equal amount of sleep in the day.

You may feel like it's better to work in the silence of the night. Whether you're studying or working, the peace in the late hours does make your job a little easier. But in the long run, this is an extremely unhealthy habit.

Our mind and body suffering from the 'night owl' routine only makes sense if we think carefully about the matter. The world is designed with a certain system in place, which is carefully created to facilitate living. Hence, going against it can hardly do us any good.

While we can't change things like the nature of the job or the employer's mind (in case you're required to work late), we can at least start by ensuring that we don't compromise our sleep for studies, work, entertainment, or anything at all. Bring back the good old 'bedtime' routine and make sure you follow it strictly. Sleeping at the same time every day for a while would automatically make the habit stronger.

Whine less, thank more

Being grateful is one of the best qualities a person can have. You can choose to be thankful for being alive or you can sulk about not having the life you want. The choice is entirely yours.

For one day, try to note down how many times you complain about something or the other. For example, the taste of your food, being overburdened with work, not getting the time to watch a new movie, etc. Unknowingly, we do tend to complain a lot and that makes us grumpy and frustrated.

Instead, if you are thankful for the good things, you feel much happier. Surely, your day isn't made of horrible events alone. There are a lot of things that can uplift your mood.

This could be your favorite song playing on the radio, your boss appreciating your work, a phone call from a friend, etc. If you try to remember these positive feelings and always count your blessings, the transformation in your mood would be unbelievable. It would almost feel like a heavy burden has been lifted off your chest.

Remember, a lot depends on your perspective. At least smaller things like the weather or a stranger's words shouldn't be able to irk you. Life gives us a lot of real challenges from time to time and we should save our energy for those, instead of whining routinely.

Be kind

Kindness costs nothing. To avoid conflicts as much as possible, saying some kind words to a person to boost his/her morale, offering a listening ear to a distressed person are all examples of daily deeds that require absolutely nothing. You just have to keep looking for ways to make this world a better place with your actions.

Your intentions are what define your inner feelings. A good deed done with a bad intention will haunt you in the future. Acts that are carried out selflessly result in a more long-lasting feeling of inner peace.

Moral corruption is one of the biggest reasons for discontentment. People who hold a lot of things against the world are dissatisfied with their conduct. If your conscience is clear, you won't have any reason to feel vengeful.

An article shared on the blog Mindset Matters discusses the effectiveness of kind behavior to feel happy (King, 2019). The opinion piece titled "Why Being Kind Is the Key to Being Happy" also gives you some tips, to begin with. These include judging less and doing thoughtful things for people without expecting anything in return.

When you perform an act of kindness just to show it off to the world, you get nothing more than a round of applause and some half-hearted compliments. Or if people do appreciate your gesture they may shower some blessings too. But other than that, there's no long-lasting pleasure derived from the activity.

Alternatively, if you act kindly out of goodwill, you will feel an inexplicable joy. Doing small acts of kindness consistently would also help improve your relationships and social standing. Inner satisfaction also leads to better performance in all areas of life.

Focus on mental health

For a minute, let's just sit back and analyze how much time we dedicate to the improvement of our mental health every day. If we find a few minutes to relax during work, we tend to check social media instead of practicing deep breathing or meditation. The bad news is, this adds to stress and anxiety.

The kind of content circulating on social media these days is far from relaxing. There's depressing news, people whining about their problems, trolls mocking the users, etc. All kinds of stressful content.

At that moment, we may not realize the toxicity of what we're reading/watching. It may seem like a fun activity and we may even have a good laugh at some of the posts. But overall, the trend is unfavorable for your mental health.

It isn't just about social media but several similar unhealthy habits that we have adopted all at once. For example, the music we listen to is mostly fast-paced so that we remain active and can work for longer. It does make us fresher momentarily but also makes it harder to calm the nerves later.

Earlier, the music played through instruments would be soulful and soothing. It induced feelings of peace and harmony. Even the lyrics in songs were thoughtful.

Even the faster songs were more melodious. Now, the noise quotient is much higher than the melody. In short, the most popular genres of modern music make it quite hard to relax.

We've only discussed a couple of examples that indicate how mental health is never a priority while choosing our habits. We could go on and on listing so many more. But the point is pretty clear: we need to change our ways to eliminate excessive stress from our lives.

Maintain a daily journal

These days, everyone is quite busy in his/her own life. It is hard to find a listening ear when you just want to pour your heart out. This results in emotions being built up inside us, causing us to feel heavy.

Of course, we have family and friends. But in adulthood, one also has to learn to deal with the issues independently. Some things are hard to share even with our close circle.

Sometimes, when we share a feeling with somebody, we do not get the response we expected. There can be disagreements, arguments, and disappointments. In such situations, opening up to somebody feels like a huge mistake.

To avoid feeling even worse than before and also avoid straining personal relationships, it is a good idea to write your feelings down. This way, you would feel lighter by letting it all out and also wouldn't have to explain yourself to anybody. The journal would be like your personal venting space.

Many popular figures in history have had the habit of maintaining a journal. From Albert Einstein to Mark Twain, the list includes names from different walks of life. The practice was more popular in ancient times but is still implemented by a significant number of people.

Once you start writing a daily journal, it does not just remain an account of the events that took place throughout the day. Gradually, you start contemplating a deeper meaning of those events. You realize patterns and become more aware of your personality.

Hence, journal writing leads to personal development as well. It makes you more philosophical and thoughtful. If used well, a habit as simple as writing your thoughts daily can bring about a drastic positive change in your life.

Speaking of maintaining a journal concerning happiness levels, in particular, it's amazing how a piece of paper can absorb all your negative feelings. It is like you have a lock and key to secure your dark side. You feel more in charge of your behavior by keeping the controversial thoughts private.

Be organized

Imagine getting late for work and as you pick a pair of trousers to wear, you cannot find a shirt to go with it. Or, let's say you're in a mood to wear a particular dress and cannot find it in the heaps of washed clothes that you didn't arrange properly. With a bad start to the day, you're likely to spend the entire day feeling annoyed.

Alternatively, let's assume you arrange your outfits for the upcoming week beforehand. You know what you're going to wear on Monday, Tuesday, and so on. These clothes are ready and hanged neatly in your wardrobe.

The second approach would not just save time but also have you excited to get ready each morning. You would happily plan your looks and feel good about it. So, this habit would bring you closer to happier living.

Being organized does not only refer to your attire or looks. Having a well-planned schedule can save you from trouble in many ways. It makes you more efficient in managing day-to-day affairs.

For example, if a person wakes up at 2 pm and realizes he has missed something important, it would certainly not be a nice feeling. There would be an embarrassment, frustration, guilt, and whatnot. On top of that, he would have lost hours of productivity which would have a cost of its own.

On the other hand, there is a person who sets an alarm for 8 am every day and wakes up on time. Not only would this result in feeling fresher and happier, but also result in a stable daily routine. Whether it is work or professional relationships, the punctuality and reliability of a fixed routine make things a lot easier in life.

Frustration often stems from the feeling of falling short of your responsibilities. Every person wants to fulfill the expectations people have from him/her. But unfortunately, not many people are ready to exercise the amount of discipline it requires.

According to a popular saying, well planned is half done. If you wish to live happily, you must first spend adequate time planning your daily routine. The routine has to be a mix of things that make you happy and the challenges that push you to do better in life.

Forgive more

Kids can have a serious fight and vow to never talk to each other. However, a few moments later, they're back to playing together as if nothing happened. Maybe this is why they tend to stay happier than the adults who keep grudges against each other for a long time.

Forgiving more is a sign of a greater tolerance level. If you're able to forgive people easily, it means that you do not believe in dwelling on past events. You want to reconcile with reality and move forward.

So, you're naturally more tolerant and patient in life. Petty quarrels cannot disturb your peace. This makes you more steadfast in facing adversities as well.

One should forgive people not for their sake but for his/her own mental peace. There is no point in holding on to something that serves no purpose in life. Staying bitter will make you feel miserable and affect your overall health.

An article titled "6 Ways Forgiveness Leads To A Happier You" shares some interesting insight about how forgiveness is linked to happiness (Woodward, 2015). It suggests that you are the one who gains something by forgiving others. It is your victory as you make others' mistakes or bad deeds irrelevant in your life.

Basically, by forgiving someone, you close a chapter. You no longer let a single event control your thoughts. You gain freedom from so many negative emotions.

Strengthen your faith

By faith, we do not mean that you should follow a certain religion or set of beliefs. We simply want to suggest that you never lose hope and stay optimistic. Your faith will help you overcome difficulties that otherwise seem too overwhelming.

Just thinking positively is insufficient to alleviate your concerns. You also have to strongly believe that the positive outcomes you have thought about will be realized. This affirmation will help avoid unnecessary stress and anxiety.

Belief is the first step towards achieving something big. It can make a rather unattainable wish seem within your reach. And once you start believing that you're capable of doing something, you've already completed half of the journey towards your destination.

You may have heard about the recently popularized art of manifestation. Not that the idea is new, but it has taken a new meaning in recent times. To describe it briefly, it is about thinking something into existence.

A major cause of anxiety is that your brain keeps telling you that something is about to go wrong. The feeling isn't rational or based on any strong logic. It is just a fear that stems from uncertainty.

Therefore, if you can assure yourself that something positive will happen, you can counter anxiety to a great extent. It is just like soothing a troubled child by making him/her believe that everything is going to be okay. Consider the anxiety a part of the personality of your inner child.

So, having a strong faith is linked to happiness in more than one way. It gives you inner peace and satisfaction. It saves you from worrying excessively about negative outcomes. And last but not the least, it increases your chances of success by making you more confident.

There is happiness in any process carried out with immense faith. When you see that your belief stood victorious against all odds, you feel even more elated. Success seems sweeter and you feel more grateful for your achievements.

Listen to your inner voice

Quite often in life, we know very well what would make us happier. An inner voice keeps telling us to follow a certain path but we feel reluctant to give in. Over time, this voice gets drowned in the noise from the outside world.

The world would tell you to dress in a certain manner, behave according to the norms set by others, adhere to tradition, etc. Stepping outside these set boundaries is often considered a crime. In other words, the world wants you to be a follower and not a leader.

Great achievers listened to their thoughts and ideas more than they listened to other people. Had they not followed their instinct, they wouldn't have done anything worthwhile in life. They would probably have a very distressing life.

An increasing number of people are also advocating talking positively to yourself. Ridiculing or belittling oneself constantly would ruin your self-esteem. Even self-deprecating humor isn't a very favorable habit when considering long-term mental health.

You see, all living things can recognize the tone that you're using with them. When dealt with kindness and love, they grow and flourish more. You can see this pattern in animals, plants, and people as well.

For some reason, when it comes to our self, we forget the positive impact that a few motivational words can have. Self-love and self-care can help you heal, shine and grow, just like loving and caring for other people or things helps them. You should always be cautious of the tone you use with yourself.

To feel healthier and happier, don't demean the ideas and thoughts in your head. You can debate the pros and cons and then decide whether you want to go ahead with an idea or just completely dismiss it. But either way, make sure you treat your thoughts with the utmost respect.

In short, there will be many situations in life where you'll have to be your moral support. Some battles are to be fought alone, without anyone's help. Therefore, always make sure that you have a cheerleader within you who is always rooting for your success.

Find an outlet for negative emotions

Some people are naturally more aggressive than others. Some tend to cry a lot at minor inconveniences. But being overly emotional should not be equated to spending an unhappy life.

The solution is to find healthy ways to emote. For example, an aggressive person can take up a sport like boxing that allows him/her to release anger. Or, someone might participate in dramas to emote freely.

Suppressing negative emotions is an unhealthy way of dealing with the problem. You either deal with them with experts' help or find a creative way to express yourself. Dwelling on unwanted thoughts and feelings can have severe consequences in the long run.

Imagine what will happen if you keep on filling gas in a tire even after it is will. Eventually, it will explode. No matter how strong the material is, nothing can endure more pressure than its capacity.

The same goes for human beings. It doesn't matter how emotionally strong you are. Having unaddressed issues will make the eventual outburst much worse.

Sometimes even talking to a friend or family member can be sufficient. At other times, people need intense physical and mental activities to vent their frustration. Either way, expressing yourself without creating more trouble with fights and confrontations enables you to remain relaxed.

Develop a sense of humor

You may have heard that laughter is the best medicine. Taking offense to everything someone else says or does will do you no good. It will only ruin your mental health and personal relationships.

If you turn every mean jibe or snide comment into a hilarious joke, you would be everyone's favorite company. Even haters would get tired of trying to irk you when they realize that you're unfazed by their remarks. On the other hand, if you keep getting worked up, people would keep poking you just to derive some sadistic pleasure from it.

So, you should be careful not to let others take advantage of your weaknesses. Even if you're deeply bothered by something, you don't have to express it in front of people who couldn't care less. Instead, you can choose to vent your anger/frustration through some healthy mediums that we have discussed in the text above.

Have a pet

Loneliness is one of the biggest reasons for the deterioration of mental health these days. We understand that the suggestion to socialize more may seem too overwhelming to some people. But one has to do something to satisfy one's emotional needs.

Taking care of a pet animal is undoubtedly a huge responsibility. It keeps you so occupied that you have little time to worry about unnecessary things. However, the wholesome company that pets provide more than makes up for this effort.

Moreover, according to science, having a pet is great for your mental health. The idea of 'animal therapy' is fast gaining popularity even in healthcare providers. Experiments showed that interacting with animals could reduce stress and anxiety for patients with serious symptoms as well.

Different animals have different effects on the owner, depending on the kind of care they need. For example, a dog realizes the changes in your mood and acts as a true companion. It is also an extremely fun play buddy.

On the other hand, a fish would just swim and look all pretty in its little pool. Yet, the owner would be worried about its food, cleanliness of the pool, protecting from little children or other animals, etc. You would selflessly love and care for it like it is your child.

So, no matter which type of pet you own, there is always a deep connection that is hard to put into words accurately. Pet lovers would agree that spending some quality time with their animal friends is quite stress-relieving. If you don't have a pet as yet and are feeling lonely or sad, you know exactly what to do.

Get creative

Adding some color to your surroundings can have a magical effect on your mood. Just a small colorful object like a pen holder or a photo frame can brighten up your work desk. Yet we choose to opt for plain, boring objects that make our workplace seem even more intimidating.

Even at home, the main focus is on practicality and not creativity. The truth is, with the latest furniture and facilities, your home is already as practical as it needs to be. What you need is a bit of a fun quotient to liven things up.

For example, instead of using a plain clay pot, you can paint it according to choice. Of course, the utility it provides would remain the same. But it would be a lot more aesthetically pleasing.

Or, if you're not too fond of too many colors, you can choose items with interesting geometric shapes. Unknowingly, whenever you look at these creative creations, you will feel happier. There are tons of ideas to explore to make your office and home seem more enjoyable.

The idea is not only restricted to home and office decor. Creative choices can be made in other things like clothing and accessories as well. This will not only make you stand out and give you a unique identity, but it will also keep you busy with a very healthy hobby.

Read more books

Reading a good book is better than reading toxic comments on social media. The former increases your knowledge and enhances your vocabulary. The latter only adds to the negative emotions.

In terms of increasing happiness, reading some fictional content is preferable as compared to nonfiction. This could be a comedy, romance, horror, or any other genre that you like. After all, you'd feel much happier reading about a fictional success story than reading the real account of someone's assassination.

Reading fiction can be like a temporary escape from reality. It takes your mind off your worries and stressful obligations. You briefly feel part of another world and start identifying with the characters in the book.

Book reading has always been encouraged as a very healthy hobby. It has extremely positive effects on your mental health and personality. Now with virtual libraries, it is even easier to get the kind of books you like.

Of course, you will have to come back to reality as soon as you close the book. But that short trip your mind takes while reading is enough to enliven your imagination. As a result, you feel happier and fresher.

Reading has also been backed by research as a way of increasing happiness. According to an article, readers are 21% less likely to experience depression (Seales, 2016). So, the fun activity surely does more than just providing entertainment.

We understand that everybody is too busy to read a lot in one go these days. It doesn't matter how much or how little read. What matters is the enjoyable experience which, by the way, will automatically make you find more time once you get used to it.

Get that adrenaline rush

Science geeks would be aware that a hormone called dopamine is responsible for us feeling happy. But did you know that adrenaline is closely related to dopamine? Here's what science says about adrenaline and happiness.

Adrenaline (or epinephrine) 'can be an antidote for boredom, malaise, and stagnation' (Bergland, 2012). Risky activities that cause fear are sometimes good for you. However, one shouldn't opt for reckless activities for the sake of an adrenaline rush.

Once in a while, you need all your senses to feel fully alive. Try stepping out of your comfort zone and do something adventurous.

As long as you take all the necessary precautions, you will only be delighted for trying something out of the box.

CHAPTER 5
THE FUTURE OF THE WORLD

Upcoming trends and the future of the world

Throughout the text, we have tried to suggest wholesome lifestyle habits. But while we're talking about scented candles and walks in the forest, the world is looking forward to flying cars and space trips. In short, it is moving further away from the simple pleasures in life.

Your imagination is undoubtedly a very powerful tool. The way you perceive things has a significant influence on your psychological wellbeing. However, your perception can never be completely alienated from reality.

Sounds confusing? Let's try to simplify this logic. You can't be in a war zone and feel tranquil. You can't be in the scorching heat of a desert and feel the chilly winds blowing in the snow-capped mountains.

There is a thin line that distinguishes euphoria from madness. Euphoria is a state of feeling incredibly happy while madness is when that happiness makes you lose touch with reality. The latter can be quite dangerous.

The best that your perception can do is make the tough situations bearable. Using mental strength, one can imagine a different scenario and thus stay motivated. Or if you're good at meditation, you may temporarily drift away to a different place mentally.

But you can't completely lose touch with reality. That would be quite disadvantageous. You have to make peace with reality and find ways to stay happy simultaneously.

If you notice carefully, nowhere in our suggestions have we mentioned making any drastic change to your life. We didn't ask you to move to a new place or change your job. Let alone asking for such life-changing steps, we didn't even ask you to try different hair colors.

The reason is that we do not wish to create a perception that happiness can only be obtained by abandoning your past self. You should endorse all parts of your journey wholeheartedly. Even the mistakes you made were necessary to bring you one step closer to achieving success in life.

So, just like we want you to proudly accept your past, we must also emphasize the importance of staying alert about future trends. You have to shape your personality according to the upcoming era.

Imagine an office secretary refusing to learn using computers because he/she is used to writing down directions manually. Such a reluctance to evolve with time would have devastating effects on one's career. The world would progress further while you would still be stuck in the past.

Keeping an eye on what's coming ahead will help you be better prepared. There are some very obvious changes in the world that we can see being materialized shortly. Here are some things that we think you should keep in mind when making plans for the coming years.

Increased technology

In the future, we can see an exponential increase in reliance on machines and technology. Every process will become increasingly mechanical. If you're not too fond of technology, then this might be the right time to change your views.

In one way or the other, we'll all have to get used to more technologically advanced solutions. We did so when the good old staircase was replaced by escalators, mobile phones replaced telephone sets and so many other innovations appeared. Going forward, there will be more advancements owing to the progress in science and technology.

In recent years, we have already seen machines replacing human beings in many fields. Mass production, agriculture, healthcare, etc, almost all areas of life have been transformed completely. Human involvement in these processes has decreased or changed from manual labor to the operation of machinery.

Social awareness

The upcoming generation is a lot more socially aware than its ancestors. Let's admit, we were never this passionate about issues such as climate change or pollution. In the future, the awareness will be even greater.

Therefore, we can expect activism and movements aimed at the resolution of some crucial issues. There would be more pressure on the global leaders to come up with better policies. Their increased awareness might make our children become the catalysts of much-needed change in the world.

Since change is an uncomfortable process, there will be some disruptions as well. For example strikes, bans, conflicts, etc. It's almost like saying things will get worse before they get better.

But at least we're confident that we're headed in the right direction. Maybe the future generation can do what we couldn't. In the wake of the rising awareness, let's cross keep our fingers crossed, and hope for the best.

Gender equality

The term may sound overused or even irrelevant to some people, but we're still far away from reaching the goal of gender equality. It is proof of the same that even some of the most progressive nations are yet to elect their first female leader. The situation in other fields is also quite similar to politics.

However, male-dominant societies are working harder than ever before to bridge the gap. Countries are showing some serious intent (to ensure no discrimination based on gender) by passing laws and spreading awareness. Although we still have a long way to go, the trend seems quite encouraging.

If you're aware of the gender inequality issues the world has faced in history, you would be quite happy with this welcome change. Those who were fortunate enough to be born in a society with equal gender roles may not understand this joy completely. Or if you're not too well aware of the history, you may want to learn more to join this happy club.

The truth is, women and transgenders never enjoyed as many rights and privileges as men in the past. There were unnecessary restrictions and unfair limitations. Even violence against 'weaker' genders was more prevalent.

Now, with more genders being recognized globally, this ancient trend of discrimination seems to be diminishing. Even the outrage when someone is treated unfairly because of gender is a positive change. After all, you can't change something if you don't find something wrong with it.

Self-reliance

People are becoming increasingly self-reliant for all their needs. Through the internet and the latest technology, it is much easier to learn new skills and ideas. There are easy-to-understand tutorials and guides in almost all popular languages.

Not only is this an interesting activity, but also a great way to save resources. Moreover, with concepts such as recycling and reusing old items gaining popularity, this facility becomes even more relevant. You can learn almost anything you want while sitting comfortably at home.

Apart from this, there are so many educational resources available on the internet. This has reduced the need to seek help from a tutor or an elder person. Again, it helps save resources and also teaches children to find solutions to their problems themselves.

Let's admit, it is a great feeling to not have to rely on anybody else for your needs. From learning a skill to fixing a broken item yourself, there is a lot of fun in virtual resources. In the coming years, more and more people will move towards DIY solutions.

The more frequent occurrence of natural disasters

You may be surprised to see this possibility being discussed along with upcoming trends. Surely, this isn't a lifestyle, nor does it seem like a pleasant topic to discuss when we're talking about happiness. But this is something that will have a strong impact on your lifestyle and your mental health.

So, we simply can't omit this discussion. With global warming and different environmental changes happening rapidly, experts believe that the world may face several unfortunate events in the coming years. No matter how harsh the reality is, we can't just choose to look away from it.

The first part of preparing for this change is to become mentally stronger. When we know that our challenges are only going to get harder, we should work on our mental strength to ensure that we're less vulnerable. You can't change everything that is happening around the world but you can at least develop some healthy coping mechanisms.

The second part is to change your day-to-day habits to make sure you're not part of the problem. Yes, many of these environmental problems are caused by humans themselves. In other words, the human race is planning its demise.

You can take small steps like avoiding the use of plastic or using organic products to become a more responsible citizen of the world. Doing something to decrease the impact of environmental damage will make you feel less guilty. By preserving the future of our upcoming generations, we can feel more peaceful and content.

Future predictions: an overview

The future is something you look forward to. The idea of tomorrow should fill you with wonder and excitement. It shouldn't make you scared about what kind of situation you're going to wake up to in the morning.

No matter how likely or unlikely an event is, the truth is that nobody can predict the future with a hundred percent accuracy. Anybody who claims to do that is either a fraud or has some supernatural powers. For a normal human being trying to identify trends and patterns in the coming years, there will always be loopholes considering the limitations of our knowledge.

The idea is to expect good things to happen but also be prepared to face adversities. In other words, to hope for the best and be prepared for the worst. Being overexcited may lead to disappointment while not looking forward to the future may make you lose interest in life. Hence, the key to happiness is a moderate approach to life.

The importance of emotional health

Emotional wellbeing is probably the most ignored aspect of an individual's health. You seldom hear that somebody didn't make it to work because he/she was feeling low. This would probably be rubbished by the peers as a lame excuse.

But is it? No, absolutely not. Depression, anxiety, or any other mental health issue can be extremely debilitating. In modern times, nobody should have the audacity to trivialize somebody's struggle with such problems.

You can't focus on any task if you're not fully there mentally. Work, personal relationships, health, everything suffers if your mind is not at ease. To expect sustainable growth in life but ignore your emotional needs is quite silly and useless.

Emotional health is different from the current mood. It is not just about how you feel at the present moment. Words like 'happy' or 'sad' aren't enough to define the broad scope of the subject.

Your emotional health reflects in your behavior, thoughts, decisions, perception, and feelings as well. It defines your personality to a great extent. It is closely linked to your overall health.

Mental health patients usually develop symptoms due to emotional setbacks in life. Suffering emotionally can weaken you mentally and physically as well. You might be surprised to know the kind of physical effects it has.

Have you ever had a heavy feeling in your chest just because you were feeling sad? Well, there is a scientific explanation for it. Here's what the experts have to say about the connection between emotions and physical health.

Being emotionally healthy is a 'fundamental aspect of fostering resilience, self-awareness, and overall contentment' according to an article shared on Healthline's website. It also states that good emotional health does not equate to permanent happiness or the absence of negative emotions. It simply means that you're better prepared to face the ups and downs of life.

The article also mentions some indicators of having emotional stability. These include being aware of your own negative emotions, realizing when you're being overly judgemental with yourself, and curiosity in terms of rationalizing your actions. If you find yourself trying to find the logic behind feeling a certain way, then it is good news.

Lastly, the article has some suggestions about improving one's emotional health. It recommends developing healthy coping mechanisms, strengthening social ties, exercising, being mindful, and getting a good night's sleep. All these habits would reduce stress make you feel calmer.

Every important health issue is related to your emotional wellbeing in one way or the other. Whether it is a heart condition or some kind of a neurological disorder, the root cause remains stress and anxiety. So, before you get to the age when the vital organs start giving you a tough time, work on becoming emotionally strong so that the battle seems easier.

CHAPTER 6
FAMOUS PEOPLE ABOUT HAPPINESS

So far, we have tried to enlighten you about the various possibilities of living a happier life. But most of the text was general discussion from our side and some science-based evidence. We haven't shared the views of the real-life heroes that people look up to.

For some reason, we value a piece of advice more when it comes from somebody we admire. It holds even more value when that person has achieved something worthwhile in life. The views also seem more credible because a person who has climbed the ladder to success can be trusted to know all the ups and downs of life quite well.

Therefore, let us now look at the views shared by some of the most famous personalities in history. Since happiness increases when you share it, we can all take a leaf out of their book and see how these people found happiness. We can already tell you that these views will also resonate with everything you have read in this book so far.

Famous Politicians

To be a politician is not an easy task. If elected, you're responsible for making decisions for so many people. If not, you never get a chance to prove your mettle.

It is also a field that requires some clever tactics and shrewd gameplay. Emotions have very little involvement in this job. Let's see how some global leaders defined happiness.

> *Happiness is when what you think, what you say, and what you do are in harmony.*

-*Mahatma Gandhi*

Mahatma Gandhi is adored by peace lovers not just in India but all over the world. He was a famous politician who held humanity above everything else. His values are appreciated by his admirers and his opponents alike.

This quote (just like many other words of wisdom he shared) gives us an important message about staying true to our words. We can't be hypocrites by saying one thing and doing something completely different. Our thoughts, words, and actions should all be in line with each other.

> *A pessimist sees the difficulty in every opportunity, an optimist sees the opportunity in every difficulty.*

-*Winston Churchill*

Imagine having such a positive outlook on life. You will be undeterred by all the difficulties in life. If anything, they'll only motivate you to try harder the next time.

Churchill led the United Kingdom in an inspirational manner during the Second World War. He also became the Prime Minister for another term later on. So, his word about handling conflicts can surely be trusted more than many others.

> *Resentment is like drinking poison and then hoping it will kill your enemies.*

-*Nelson Mandela*

Who doesn't know Nelson Mandela? The man was among the biggest proponents of peace and equality in the world. The former South African President won the hearts of people all over the world with his exceptional leadership skills.

Remember when we suggested being more forgiving for greater happiness? These words by Nelson Mandela reiterate the same idea. Resentment does more harm to you than it does to the people you hold grudges against.

> *'The ancient Greek definition of happiness was the full use of your powers along lines of excellence.'*

— *John F. Kennedy*

So, believing this definition presented by JFK, happiness lies in living efficiently. One should work as hard as he/she can. Moreover, attention should be paid to enhancing your set of skills over time.

Sports Personalities

Sports is not just a mode of entertainment. For some people, it is their entire life. Playing or watching sports brings joy to so many people around the world.

But along with thrill and excitement, it also causes pain and sorrow. You can't truly succeed until you learn to handle your defeats well. A sportsman needs a lot of hard work, courage, resilience, and belief to achieve his goals.

> *If my mind can conceive it, and my heart can believe it — then I can achieve it.*

-Muhammad Ali

Muhammad Ali wasn't just an amazing boxer. He was quite an inspirational personality outside the ring as well. His words were always full of courage and passion.

This particular quote speaks volumes about his positive thinking. You have to perceive success before you can achieve it. Once you start thinking positively, everything else will automatically fall into place.

> *Worrying gets you nowhere.*

-Usain Bolt

What do we achieve by getting worried? Nothing at all. We couldn't agree more with this statement of Usain Bolt.

Bolt is one of the fastest athletes in recent history. He says he never doubts himself and knows his capabilities. This strong belief in himself has brought him an immense amount of success in his career.

> *"I've missed more than 9,000 shots in my career. I've lost almost 300 games. Twenty-six times I've been trusted to take the game-winning shot and missed. I've failed over and over and over again in my life. And that is why I succeed."*

—*Michael Jordan*

Just keep trying again and again. There is no reason that success won't eventually come your way. You just have to keep your faith strong.

Jordan's description inspires you to try at least one more time. His success speaks volumes about his determination. So, we should just be proud of ourselves for never giving up and that alone will make us feel happier about life.

> *"Just believe in yourself. Even if you don't pretend that you do and, and some point, you will."*

—<u>Venus Williams</u>

Both Williams sisters have enjoyed their kind of success in the world of tennis. While Serena has enjoyed more achievements, Venus has fought hard to make a mark of her own. This is probably why her words contain so much wisdom.

When worry takes over, try to soothe yourself with positive thoughts. Believe that everything will eventually be okay. This will keep you calmer and stress-free.

Celebrities and entertainment personalities

The glitzy world of glamour has its challenges. There's competition, stress, and the pressure of being in the public eye all the time. One needs to hold the nerves and try different things to feel truly happy.

> *I am my own experiment. I am my own work of art.*

-Madonna

Madonna is one fierce lady from the entertainment industry. With millions of fans around the world, the singer never fails to impress. Whether it is her music or her bold words, she has a unique way of winning hearts.

Creative people view happiness quite differently. They take pride in their work and feel happy when it is appreciated. It is the biggest dream of any creative artist that people would love the work that they have done so passionately.

> *I am not interested in money. I just want to be wonderful.*

-Marilyn Monroe

Here's another successful person telling us that personal growth and feelings matter more than material gains. Happiness cannot be achieved by running after money or fame. You will find happiness in doing what you love.

> *Life is a tragedy when seen in close-up, but a comedy in long-shot.*

-Charlie Chaplin

Humor will get you through a lot of difficult things in life. It makes the situation lighter and keeps you happier in the long run. Charlie Chaplin has taught us the same.

CONCLUSION

In the end, we must once again reiterate that life requires you to find happiness for yourself. Your comfort, passion, wishes, and everything else that is necessary for you to feel happy, matters the most. More than understanding life, try to focus on enjoying it.

The problem is, we want to decipher the meaning of everything in life. But the truth is, we're not supposed to know everything. Certain mysteries are meant to remain unsolved.

For example, you can't predict how long a person is going to live or what will happen to him/her after death. You can't know what the weather will be like on the same date next year. In short, you will never have all the answers to life.

Moreover, we always want to remain one step ahead of everyone else. If not another person, then we try to compete with nature by defeating time. We simply forget that life is not a race with others but a unique journey of our own.

Being far-sighted is a good thing. It lets you plan more efficiently. But being too curious about the future will not let you enjoy the present moment.

Similarly, the wish to acquire more knowledge is one of the best qualities for a person to have. However, being over-inquisitive causes stress and worry. The idea is to never go overboard or become obsessed with a certain concept.

There is a huge difference between theory and practical life.

The theory would simply tell you to 'stay happy'. Practical life would make you realize how hard this goal is.

Reading a manual is much simpler than performing an action. No matter how clear the directions are, doing something for the first time has its challenges. Ironically in terms of life, the first chance also happens to be our last chance.

The idea of the last chance at something often fills you with apprehension and anxiety. You don't want to mess it up. You forget everything else and try to give it your best shot.

While trying to focus on the fact that this is our last chance, we often forget that it is our first one too. We refuse to give ourselves the margin of error that is usually allowed for first attempts. But remember, it is okay to not be perfect at something that you are trying for the first time.

From birth to death, life is a matter of trial and error. If we let failures destroy our confidence, we will never be able to attain true happiness. Once we wrap our heads around this fact, it will be easier to digest the defeats we face.

Elbert Hubbard once suggested to not take life too seriously as nobody makes it out alive anyway. And we couldn't help but agree how hilariously apt this is. When you know that you have limited time on this planet, why not try to use it well and be happy?

For a change, don't wait for better times and live each moment like it is the most perfect one. Treat it as a unique opportunity to experience something new. Forget about the consequences or the fear of making an error.

To live freely will bring you happiness. If you like going out, there are so many different places for you to explore. If you prefer remaining indoors, you can create a small world of your own inside your home.

The universe holds something for everybody. We spoil our happiness by overthinking everything. After reading this book, we hope you try to keep it simple and succeed in finding true happiness.

REFERENCES

Anderson, L. (2019). Coorie: What You Need to Know About the Scottish Lifestyle Trend. SD Publishing.

Australia's Lifestyle and Culture - Tourism Australia. (n.d.). Retrieved January 23, 2021, from https://www.australia.com/en/facts-and-planning/about-australia/the-aussie-way-of-life.html

Bakken, S. (2020). Friluftsliv: Everything You Need to Know About the Nordic Lifestyle of Friluftsliv. SD Publishing.

Bergland, C. (2012, November 29). The Neurochemicals of Happiness. Retrieved January 24, 2021, from https://www.psychologytoday.com/us/blog/the-athletes-way/201211/the-neurochemicals-happiness

Bloom, L. B. (2020, October 29). Ranked: The 20 Happiest Countries In The World. Retrieved January 23, 2021, from https://www.forbes.com/sites/laurabegleybloom/2020/03/20/ranked-20-happiest-countries-2020/#:~:text=The%20U.S.%20ranked%20number%2018,the%20first%20World%20Happiness%20Report.

Commisceo Global Consulting Ltd. (2020, January 1) Australia - Language, Culture, Customs and Etiquette. Retrieved from https://commisceo-global.com/resources/country-guides/Australia-guide

Conci, P. (2019, January 16). Why Are Latin Americans Happier than Their GDP Would Suggest? Retrieved January 23, 2021, from https://blogs.iadb.org/ideas-matter/en/latin-americans-happier-gdp-suggest/

Future lifestyles in Europe and in the United States in 2020. (2013, December). Retrieved January 24, 2021, from https://espas.secure.europarl.europa.eu/orbis/sites/default/files/generated/document/en/10%20EFFLA%20Study%20-%20Tikka%20-%20Wevolve%20-%20Life%20styles.pdf

Holiday, R. (2016). Daily Stoic: 366 Meditations on Self-Mastery, Perseverance and Wisdom: Featuring New Translations of Seneca, Marcus Aurelius and Epictetus. Penguin Publishing Group.

Jansen, T. (2020). Cocooning Lifestyle: Enjoying Happy and Safe Times at Home. BN Publishing.

Jansen, T. (2020). *Niksen: The Power of Doing Nothing*. SD Publishing.

King, L. (2019, August 10). Why Being Kind Is the Key to Being Happy. Retrieved January 24, 2021, from https://medium.com/mindset-matters/why-being-kind-is-the-key-to-being-happy-d9ae760906

Kogan, N. (n.d.). The magic of a good night's sleep. Retrieved January 24, 2021, from https://www.happier.com/blog/the-magic-of-sleep/

Lamothe, C. (2019, June 14). How to Build Good Emotional Health (1164345683 873859730 T. J. Legg, Ed.). Retrieved January 24, 2021, from https://www.healthline.com/health/emotional-health

Oaklander, M. (n.d.). Science Says Your Pet Is Good for Your Mental Health. Retrieved January 24, 2021, from https://time.com/collection/guide-to-happiness/4728315/science-says-pet-good-for-mental-health/

Pobjie, B. (2017, April 27). The 10 most Australian values that make Australia so valuable. Retrieved January 23, 2021, from https://www.abc.net.au/news/2017-04-28/these-are-our-core-australian-values/8476902

Popcorn, F. (1992). *The Popcorn report*. Milsons Point, New South Wales: Random House Australia.

Preidt, R. (2019, April 11). Science Says: Smiling Helps You Get Happy. Retrieved January 24, 2021, from https://www.webmd.com/mental-health/news/20190411/science-says-smiling-helps-you-get-happy#:~:text=The%20researchers'%20conclusion%3A%20Facial%20expressions,in%20the%20journal%20Psychological%20Bulletin.

Reynolds, G. (2018, May 02). Even a Little Exercise Might Make Us Happier. Retrieved January 13, 2021, from https://www.nytimes.com/2018/05/02/well/move/even-a-little-exercise-might-make-us-happier.html#:~:text=Small%20amounts%20of%20exercise%20could,of%20exercise%20may%20be%20helpful.

Seales, J. (2016, November 23). 10 Reasons Reading Makes You Feel Happier, In Case You Need Another Excuse To Buy Books. Retrieved January 24, 2021, from https://www.bustle.com/articles/194838-10-reasons-reading-makes-you-feel-happier-in-case-you-need-another-excuse-to-buy-books#:~:text=Books%20Can%20Open%20Your%20Mind,Journal%20of%20Applied%20Social%20Psychology.

Sheikh, A. (2020, March 23). Pakistan is the Happiest Country in South Asia. Retrieved January 24, 2021, from https://pk.mashable.com/pakistan/2062/pakistan-is-the-happiest-country-in-south-asia

Telford, O. (2017). Hygge: Discovering the Danish art of happiness -- how to live cozily and enjoy life's simple pleasures. Olivia Telford.

Woodward, C. (2015, May 19). 6 Ways Forgiveness Leads To A Happier You. Retrieved January 24, 2021, from https://wallstreetinsanity.com/6-ways-forgiveness-leads-to-a-happier-you/#:~:text=Forgiveness%20means%20you%20win%20%E2%80%94%20yes,you%20are%20the%20ultimate%20winner.

OTHER BOOKS BY SOFIE BAKKEN

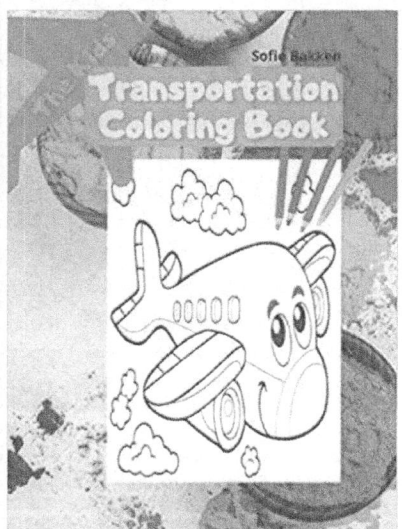

ABOUT SOFIE BAKKEN

Sofie is married and has two children. She lives with her family in a European country. During the last years, she got more and more interested in de-stressing her life and improving her life quality. She stumbled upon some Nordic European lifestyles that she examined thoroughly. Her studies also led her to the topic of longevity. She enjoys her family, nature as well as cooking and coloring.

Made in the USA
Monee, IL
03 May 2026

49438708R00080